W9-CCN-856

FROM THE LIBRARY OF

David Tillman

Magnet Marketing

---- ✧ ----

The Ultimate Strategy for Attracting and Holding Customers

John R. Graham
with
Steven J. Bennett

John Wiley & Sons, Inc.

New York • Chichester • Brisbane • Toronto • Singapore

In recognition of the importance of preserving what has been written, it is a policy of John Wiley & Sons, Inc. to have books of enduring value published in the United States printed on acid-free paper, and we exert our best efforts to that end.

Copyright © 1991 John R. Graham and Steven J. Bennett
Published by John Wiley & Sons, Inc.
All rights reserved. Published simultaneously in Canada.

Reproduction or translation of any part of this work beyond that permitted by Section 107 or 108 of the 1976 United States Copyright Act without the permission of the copyright owner is unlawful. Requests for permission or further information should be addressed to the Permissions Department, John Wiley & Sons, Inc.

This publication is designed to provide accurate and authoritative information in regard to the subject matter covered. It is sold with the understanding that the publisher is not engaged in rendering legal, accounting or other professional service. If legal advice or other expert assistance is required, the services of a competent professional person should be sought *From a Declaration of Principles jointly adopted by a Committee of the American Bar Association and a Committee of Publishers.*

Library of Congress Cataloging-in-Publication Data

Graham, John R. (John Rushton), 1931-
    Magnet marketing : the ultimate strategy for attracting and holding customers / by John R. Graham with Steven J. Bennett.
        p.   cm.
    Includes bibliographical references.
    ISBN 0-471-52648-7
    1. Marketing—Management.   2. Customer service.   3. Customer satisfaction.   I. Bennett. Steven J., 1951-   .   II. Title.

    HF5415.13.G68 1991
    658.8'02—dc20   90-38120

Printed in the United States of America

91 92 10 9 8 7 6 5 4 3 2 1

For my wife
Mary E. Weafer

Her Influence—beyond measure.
Her faith—beyond bounds.
Her standards—beyond compromise.
Her judgment—beyond question.

Acknowledgments

———— ✧ ————

Magnet Marketing grew out of the firm belief that a strong point of view is required for effective marketing and sales. What appeared to be missing in the literature was a concept that met the demands of business in the decade of the 1990s.

Over the years, the staff of Graham Communications has had a clearly enunciated philosophy of marketing and sales. In the final analysis, the marketing task is to draw the customer to you —like a magnet. Instead of trying to find the needle in the haystack, the job is to provide a way for the needle to find you.

As we shared our thinking with clients and others, there was an enthusiastic response. "Of course. That makes sense." In effect, we were providing a conceptual framework for marketing and sales programs.

Over a period of time, we extended our thinking—our marketing philosophy—to the readers of several dozen business publications. The response was somewhat overwhelming. What we considered to be a commonsense approach was often viewed as quite revolutionary, since the prevailing practice is to "go out and get the customer."

As time went on and more articles were published, several friends and associates urged us to be cautious. "Don't give away your secrets." Since one of the cornerstones of "magnet marketing" is the need for customer education, we ignored such counsel. We believe that one of the major faults of business today is an attitude of unnecessary and inappropriate secrecy. Sharing ideas will do more than anything else to revitalize American business!

When it dawned on me that maybe all this could become a book—a way to make the commitment to customer education even further, we began searching for an agent (isn't that what a would-be author is supposed to do?). After talking with several business book specialists, we chose Mike Snell of Truro, Massachusetts. Thanks to Mike, a bright, creative and incredibly hard working young man came along. Steve Bennett took my words and ideas and molded them into a highly focused book—*Magnet Marketing*. Working with Steve is a special reward of this project.

When all is said and done, it takes a publisher to make a book possible. Editor John Mahaney of John Wiley & Sons gave us a long leash. I can't imagine a better person to work with. Even more important, I will always have a special place in my heart for John because he published my first book.

But *Magnet Marketing* would never have become a reality had it not been for the talented staff of Graham Communications. Although privately, I suspect, they may think that I'm somewhat "off-the-wall," they accept and tolerate me with both grace and encouragement. I am grateful for their generosity—and patience.

Our clients are noblest of all. Graham Communications is indeed fortunate to be able to work with outstanding people. They do far more than keep us in business. They allow us to put "magnet marketing" to work. They deserve both our thanks and our gratitude.

Finally, a word must be said about someone who is perhaps the best "magnet marketer" of all—my eight year-old daughter, Johnice Graham. At a very young age, she has developed an incredible optimism about life. Watch out when she hits the 21st century! If there was inspiration for this book, the credit must go to her. She deserves it.

John R. Graham
Quincy, Massachusetts

Contents

✧

Memorandum

──────── ✧ ────────

To: Business people who have a gnawing
      feeling that something is wrong...

From: John Graham

Re: Control of your destiny
──────────────────────────-
If you're the type that doesn't like waiting
for punchlines, here's something to whet your
appetite:

Fact: Less than 10 percent of your customers
go by price alone. What do they want? ESS:

* <u>Enthusiasm</u>. People want to feel good. That's
  why they respond so well to the positive,
  can-do-it person. The magic word in business
  is "Sure." That's what the customer wants to
  hear. You may not know how you're going to
  get it done, but the challenge is exhilarat-
  ing—and your customers sense your desire to
  accomplish the impossible.

* <u>Solutions</u>. What's missing in most business
  people? <u>Ideas, Ideas, Ideas</u>. The best way to
  get the business is to think up innovative

ideas. Dull is devastating when it comes to increasing sales. Solve customer problems, share information, apply your expertise, and you have power. Squeeze out every ounce of creativity you can find between your ears!

• Service. But not what we commonly think of as service. Not just an 800 number. And certainly not mindless "smile therapy." Customer service means anticipating customer needs. It means leading the way. It means being a consultant. These are the only ways to become indispensable to your customers. If you're perceived as a partner, you'll have a friend for life, someone you can count on no matter how tough the times or the competition.

Practice ESS and you'll create a natural pull that brings customers to your doorstep. Today, tomorrow, and deep into the future—which is what magnet marketing is all about. Sound good? You, too, can join the ranks of business who have taken control over their companies' destiny. Just flip the page and keep reading—this book will arm you with all the techniques you need to smooth out the peaks and valleys, maintain a steady flow of sales, and gain a competitive advantage in the marketplace. Besides, it practices what it preaches—you'll find enthusiasm, fresh ideas, and above all service. Think of it as your portable marketing and sales consultant, ready to help you out at every turn of the road. That's ESS in action.

Introduction

──────── ✧ ────────

A Quiet Revolution in Marketing

*Graham's Law: If you think you know
everything about selling, why aren't you
selling everything?*

Warning. If you're looking for the latest fad in marketing, you'll be disappointed with this book. It doesn't offer any one-minute solutions. It doggedly avoids any mention of "excellence." It doesn't teach you how to thrive on chaos. It contains no magic seeds for renewal. And it won't help you swim with sharks, tuna, flounder, or any other creatures of the deep.

Rather, *Magnet Marketing* will put you back in touch with the only sure-fire ticket to success: Common Business Sense. The techniques offered in *Magnet Marketing* can be used in retail, manufacturing, service, and any other types of businesses.

More important than what you make or sell is what you are willing to do to improve your business.

If you are willing to bare your soul and admit weaknesses in your marketing and selling operations, you've taken the first step towards significant change. If you are willing to establish realistic goals—and support them with a commitment from top management—you've taken the next. And the third and final step? Read on. The following pages provide you with a soup-to-nuts program for analyzing your current marketing effectiveness and developing techniques that will cultivate long-term customers.

Chapters 1 and 2 explore why traditional sales and marketing tactics fail in today's highly competitive business environment, while Chapter 3 develops a new theory of what motivates customers and builds total customer loyalty.

From Chapter 4 you can learn how to assess your current marketing efforts, and how to establish marketing goals that will enable you to achieve your financial targets. Chapters 5 through 7 cover the core customer cultivation techniques of a magnet marketing program: self-promotion, media relations, and advertising.

Chapter 8 describes the importance of customer education, while Chapter 9 focuses on techniques for keeping customers and generating repeat business. Chapter 10 discusses the application of magnet marketing in the area of professional services. Chapter 11 focuses on the application of survival marketing techniques during tough times.

At this point, you'll have learned about the key components of a magnet marketing program, and how they can be woven into a strategy for success. The book then shifts to the need for complementing magnet marketing with a strong sales effort. Chapters 12 and 13 focus on the sales process—what often goes wrong and how to use the power of sales authority to close deals. This brings the book full circle, to the earlier chapters that describe the problem with marketing and sales today, and how they can be solved.

It also brings you to the point where you need to consider the dynamics of change in your organization; while you will no doubt be convinced that magnet marketing is a blueprint for your company's success, you will have to convince others in your organization that the traditional methods of selling products and services is no longer valid to meet the pressures of the 1990s. Chapters 14 and 15 describe the kinds of obstacles you may have to overcome and provides proven techniques for vaulting over the hurdles. Chapter 16 offers insights into the challenges that all businesses will face in their quest to grow and prosper in the new decade.

For a summary of the key magnet marketing techniques, read the Epilogue—you might even want to copy it and keep it by your desk to remind you of the rich array of actions that you and your company can take to attract and hold customers.

Finally, take a look at the Devil's Marketing Dictionary—you just might find some words that you should eliminate from your vocabulary before they become declassé.

ON YOUR WAY

Before launching into the program, be aware that magnet marketing is not a panacea.

- If you're bleeding from the neck, get some emergency help. Magnet marketing is a business philosophy, not a solution for every short-term crisis.

- If your company is plagued by deep-seated organizational problems, solve them first. Magnet marketing only works when the company has the internal strength to attract loyal customers.

- If your company operates as a collection of fiefs, it must find a way for the feudal lords to share their power. Magnet marketing entails everyone working in concert towards the beat of a single drummer—the customer.

Above all, don't waste your time reading this book if you're looking for a paint-by-numbers solution to your marketing or sales problems. Marketing is an approach to doing business that must be tailored to your company. This requires an investment of time and energy on everyone's part to make it work.

What kind of rewards are you likely to reap with magnet marketing? Like everything else in life, that depends what you're willing to put on the table. As a marketeer who hasn't had to make a cold call in ten years, you can take my word for it that this is a *safe* bet.

———— ✧ ————

Rethinking Two Old Professions

Differentiating Marketing and Sales

Graham's Law: If you have a "Sales and Marketing" department, you are undoubtedly doing a lot of other things backwards, too.

BUSINESS AS USUAL

A team of archeologists digging in the Middle East once uncovered a wealth of buried clay tablets. Surely, they thought, the writing on the tablets would greatly enhance our understanding of an ancient civilization. To everyone's surprise, though, the tablets represented invoices, bills, dunning notices, and other mundane paperwork from centuries earlier. It was as if the business office of a major corporation had gotten stuck in time.

Today, our dot matrix printers hammer away at multipart carbonless forms rather than sheets of stone; and we offer an infinitely more sophisticated array of products and services. In a sense, though, many modern companies are stuck in their own time warp. They continue to practice turn-of-the-century sales techniques that are no longer effective in today's marketplace.

Take cold calling, for example. Since the invention of door-to-door selling, every company has expected its salespeople to make cold calls. Over and over again, sales managers tell their troops, "Go get the customers." Cold calling is more than a mere tradition—it's a passion and the way of life for most of America's salespeople! It's also a waste of time and the single greatest reason that salespeople fail and companies do not meet their full potential.

Selling is not a matter of luck, of catching a prospect who happens to be interested in buying from you. Nor is it a matter of getting your foot in the door and turning on the "gift of gab." That approach might have worked in the days when people hawked vacuum cleaners and stainless steel pots and pans. Today, selling is an art that enables the salesperson to be in the right place at the right time—when the customer is ready and eager to buy.

The chief reason that salespeople have difficulty these days is that their companies do not understand the role of marketing in the sales process. Too many companies, even rather sophisticated ones, see "sales and marketing" as two sides of the same

3

coin. They lump "sales and marketing" into one division, one department, or one functional area. In fact, most companies use "sales" and "marketing" quite interchangeably.

There are two problems with this "sales and marketing" approach. Firstly, the words "sales" and "marketing" are not synonyms. Each has its own unique role to play. Secondly, let's set the record straight. It is never "sales and marketing." It is always "marketing and sales," since marketing must always precede sales.

Marketing has a very special job. Its task is to create the right buying environment so that customers are primed when salespeople call. The goal of marketing is to create leads for the sales force. The job of the salesperson is making the sale, closing the deal. But this generally doesn't happen. Instead, salespeople are goaded into finding their own leads! What a waste of time and talent—and lost sales.

Another result of confusing marketing and sales functions is the time- honored tradition of price cutting. Every company has, at some point, said, "We want the business, so we'll take a bath on this deal to get our feet in the door. If we don't get the price down, we'll lose the sale."

The problem with such "loss leaders," of course, is that the exception becomes the rule. In order to get the business, they cut the price. Again, and again, and again. Companies then get used to operating on increasingly slimmer margins, creating the need for ever higher sales volume to compensate for the losses. The truth is, if the company really had something worth buying, and it's marketing people did their jobs, the firm wouldn't have to give up a dime.

Unfortunately, when it comes to the budget, the sales department gets the lion's share of dollars and marketing is left with a few bucks to come up with a catalog or brochure that touts a product or service. Rarely is their money earmarked for customer cultivation, which is the only way to grow and prosper over the long haul.

In short, businesses simply can't continue to operate as they did in the past, ignoring the need to prime customers for a sale long before the salesperson knocks on the door. Let's take a look at how the world has changed and why a new set of tools is needed for companies to achieve success in the 1990s and beyond.

THE MODERN CHALLENGES OF SELLING

In the past, techniques like cold calling and price slashing served companies well. But the world is zipping along too fast today and time has become a precious commodity. Who can afford to respond to an endless series of cold calls? Most of us don't even have enough time in an eight-hour day to finish what we have to do, let alone listen to hype about a new service or widget that will make us happier, healthier, or wealthier. Also, who wants to listen to someone trying to persuade them to do business with a company they've never heard of until the salesperson walked through the door?

Today, customers are not just put off by such intrusions into their work day and private lives; they're angry. Under such conditions, what are the chances of making the sale with a cold call? Slim, to say the least.

Another factor that has rendered traditional approaches to sales obsolete is the vast increase in global competition. The number of new players in just about every field is growing by leaps and bounds. This means companies can't afford inefficient "shotgun" techniques that "bag" customers on a hit or (usually) miss basis. "Selling" is synonymous with "timing." You had better be there when the customer is ready to sign on the dotted line or else someone else will beat you to the punch. How many times have you heard a customer say something like, "Gee, too bad you weren't around last week—we would have done business with you." It's impossible to synchronize with your customers by randomly "touching base."

The shotgun approach to selling products and services is also far too expensive in today's economic climate. Much of the money spent on "blasting" the marketplace is wasted on people who have little predisposition to buy your product or service. With today's competitive pressures, only companies that run leanly and efficiently will come out winners in the battle for the market share.

Despite the fact that new marketing and sales techniques are needed—and available—for a changing world, most companies still use the old standbys. And the results are telling:

- *Lower than possible sales levels.* Few companies really achieve the sales figures they should. And we're not talking about some artificially inflated target that management poses to scare people into performing. We're talking about real and steady growth in good and bad economic times alike.

- *A frustrated sales force.* The high turnover in sales departments today is symptomatic of using outdated approaches to marketing and sales. So is a constant reshuffling of sales territories. What are the most common laments of salespeople these days?

  "We don't have enough leads."

  "No one knows our company."

  "We're getting killed because our prices are too high."

  What is a company's typical response? Make more calls. Find the right sales technique. Take the right seminar. Do something to improve your performance—particularly your closing rate! Sadly, though, browbeaten quota-driven salespeople don't last over the long haul.

Since hope springs eternal in any salesperson's heart, they wander off to greener pastures.

- *A phantom marketing department.* In most companies, marketing is a "closet" where you get the brochures and catalogs, rather than a function that creates a positive buying environment. This places the task of selling the company, the company's products, or the company's services squarely on the heads of the salespeople. In other words, it shifts a critical task to the *wrong* people.

- *Loss of competitive strengths.* If you're not marketing and selling with techniques for the 1990s, you can bet someone else is, or will be soon.

- *A victim mind set.* Many companies come to expect that their business is like a roller coaster and that their performance is largely determined by external conditions. "Gee, we're very sensitive to interest rates. Interest rates are up, so we're headed for a down turn. Better 'batten down the hatches'." Such thinking becomes a self-fulfilling prophecy and often leads to needless layoffs and diminished financial performance. Worse, it obscures the fact that the real cause of the peaks and valleys is an inability to create a positive buying environment, regardless of conditions in the outside world.

  Good companies with good products and services can sell under any conditions because they have developed a special edge over their competitors—they have become "the vendor of choice" in the minds of their customers. Fueled by customer loyalty, they can weather any storm and come out on top. When you have customers who will stick with you through thick and thin, you've got it all.

Your company has probably experienced at least one of the problems described in this chapter, maybe more. Why are these problems so pervasive in business today? In Chapter 2, we'll investigate the root causes of the most common problems in sales and marketing today. Be honest and open as you read them and acknowledge how they apply to your company. You can then choose between continuing with the *status quo* or following our proven path to increased sales, a stronger competitive position, improved stability, and the kind of long-term profitability that comes from taking a customer orientation.

Challenging the Traditional Wisdom

Why Willy Can't Sell

Graham's Law: Attending sales seminars will always boost sales—for the speaker.

His name was Dave Singleman. And he was eighty four years old, and he'd drummed merchandise in thirty one states. And old Dave, he'd go up to his room, y'understand, put on his green velvet slippers—I'll never forget—and pick up his phone and call the buyers, and without ever leaving his room, at the age of eighty four, he made his living. And when I saw that, I realized that selling was the greatest career a man could want. 'Cause what could be more satisfying than to be able to go, at the age of eighty four, into twenty or thirty different cities, and pick up a phone, and be remembered and loved and helped by so many different people? Do you know? When he died—and by the way he died the death of a salesman, in his green velvet slippers in the smoker of the New York, New Haven, and Hartford going into Boston—when he died, hundreds of salesmen and buyers were at his funeral. Things were sad on a lotta trains for months after that. In those days, there was personality in it, Howard. There was respect, and comradeship, and gratitude in it. Today, it is all cut and dried, and there's no chance for bringing friendship to bear—or personality. You see what I mean? They don't know me anymore. (*Death of a Salesman*)

WHAT'S WRONG WITH SALES TODAY?
IT'S ALL CUT AND DRIED

No one said it better than Willy Loman: personality, while it still counts, doesn't sell products. Customers need to be primed so they're ready to buy and that only happens when salespeople and marketing people work in concert.

Sadly, the ghost of Willy Loman still haunts the sales offices of many companies today. Salespeople are confused by the fact that they go through the motions, yet nothing happens. Take a midwestern manufacturer of medical supplies whose sales were stagnant because of a deadly combination of the cost-cutting fever sweeping the health care industry and heavy pressure from competitors. The vice president asked us what could be done to stop the erosion, so we flew down and met with the entire sales force in an attempt to find out exactly what was happening in the field. Here are the highlights of our initial meeting:

Question:	How does your marketing department support your sales efforts?
Answer:	Blank stares. What marketing department? We have a sales department!
Question:	How do you connect with customers?
Answer:	Each sales rep targets a hospital and shows up at 9:00 A.M. unannounced, then starts running down the docs. If a doctor is in surgery or tied up with a patient, the rep goes on to the next doctor, until he's wandered the entire hospital in search of someone who will listen to him. If he's lucky, by the end of the day he might make one connection.
Question:	How do you follow up with the doctors who wanted additional information?
Answer:	We wait until the last day of the month, then make a follow-up call or send out literature.

Question: If a physician saw you on the second day of the month and expressed an interest in one of your products, would you wait until the end of the month before following up?

Answer: Sure! It's much more efficient to do the follow up at one time.

What these people failed to realize was that each physician is driven by a unique set of needs. Money. Time. Ego. And so forth. The thought never occurred to them that by tailoring their approach to a doctor's individual style and needs, they could drastically improve their sales rate. Instead, they chose to fly on autopilot, ignoring opportunities for attracting customers. Unconsciously, they made the biggest mistake of all because they saw themselves as "professionals," they assumed that their style and their manner of selling was all-important.

These people assumed that sales are made by playing the numbers game—cold calling or "sales roulette." In the Introduction, we commented that cold calling is a time-honored, though highly ineffective technique for making sales, and a sure sign of deep-seated trouble. Let's look a little closer at the reasons.

First, what's the message when salespeople call and say, "Are you familiar with our company?" or "I would like to introduce myself and the XYZ company."? They are publicizing the fact that their firms have no marketing programs.

Even nationally known corporations fall into the cold calling trap. These are the salespeople who assume that because they are from one of the "Fortune 1000," the customer will be so impressed that he'll rush to stop everything just to talk to them at length on the phone, or that he'll interrupt his schedule to make room for an appointment. They have been led to believe that their company's prestige is sufficient to get the customer's attention and time. Such ill-conceived arrogance is both a myth and is inappropriate today.

Of course, there are times when the cold call strikes it rich—make enough calls and you'll make a hit. That's the theory. But what about the 99 who said "No" or who didn't take the call? Are they written off and forgotten? Of course. Don't stop to think about the possibilities. There's no time to give attention to what those 99 may need in the future. Just move on to the next name and number. Do it enough and you'll make a sale. "It's all in the numbers," says the sales manager.

Then, there's that endless stream of cold calling salespeople who come through the door asking for "only 20 minutes of your time." Why should anyone stop and see a stranger? There's also the salesperson who "just drops by" and leaves a business card. What a waste of time, effort, and money! "I was in the area," they all say. Who cares? And who wants to do business with a salesperson who has nothing better or more constructive to accomplish than going from office to office? They aren't in sales. They're canvassers.

Our experience indicates that firms relying on cold calling fit this profile:

- They do not have an overall marketing strategy. Their approach is simply to "make sales." They live from day to day and from gimmick to gimmick.

- They suffer from severe swings in sales figures.

- When sales lag, they dream up "sales contests" to try to prod the sales force to be more aggressive.

- They experience a high turnover in sales personnel. Demoralized and defeated, their people leave quickly. These are the companies that run ad after ad in the classifieds trying to snare the gullible.

- They have little respect for their product or service and even less regard for their customers. Getting the sale is more important than anything else. They rely on sales techniques rather than customer-building strategies.

- They demonstrate that they do not know how to utilize the talents and abilities of a sales force.

- They have sales managers who are successful (for a period of time) in pushing, shoving, browbeating, intimidating, and prodding (all disguised as motivating) their people to make more—and tougher—calls. These managers are paid big bucks and quickly move on to the next company that is looking for the pot of gold at the end of the rainbow. Unfortunately, there are plenty of them around.

All this is without question a serious indictment of cold calling, a technique still relied upon by thousands and thousands of businesses. In fact, cold calling is a fairly good barometer of the state of the economy. When things get tighter, you can expect more and more cold calls.

Even though cold calling may get this month's or this year's figures up, the long-term effects are negative because the process fails to build lasting customer relationships. Nine times out of 10, buyers never hear from the company again once the sale is made—until it's time to sell them something else.

If a company is interested in long-term success and building a solid, loyal customer base, then a totally different approach is required. It is one that emphasizes the importance of the company's values regarding its products and services and its relationship to customers. Most important, it is one that recognizes that a company must work at developing customers so that it deserves the sales it makes. A sale in this view is not a mark on a sales manager's chalkboard, but a statement of the company's commitment to creating customers.

This brings us back to the point stressed in the Introduction: if you want sales to grow, no matter what might be happening in the economy, and if you want to prosper in spite of your competition, then you'd better give marketing a high priority. In the long run, effective marketing is the only way for you to achieve your financial goals. In the next chapters, you'll learn about a common sense approach to marketing that any firm in any industry can put to immediate use. First, though, let's take a closer look at the functions of marketing, and examine why most companies do such a poor job of marketing their goods or services.

COMMON MARKETING MISTAKES

Every company has only one job and that's to make itself stand out in the marketplace. A business must work hard to differentiate itself from its competitors. Specifically, it must do everything possible to have its customers and prospects view it as "one of a kind."

But when you get right down to it, most companies aren't very glamorous. Their products and services are rather ordinary. If you're honest with yourself, you'll have to admit that you're just about as good as your competition. Maybe a little better here, but not quite as good there.

Going head-to-head with competitors day after day isn't the answer. Spending time beating the other guy away from the customer's door by cutting your price is self-defeating. Trying to be every place at the right moment is impossible. It's also discouraging. If you don't use marketing to influence what customers think of you, your company, and your products or services, they will come to their own conclusions. Beyond a shadow of a doubt, their perceptions will be inaccurate and even wrong. Worse yet, they will not even think of you at all.

All this creates the vital need for every company to spend considerable time, effort, and money positioning itself in the marketplace. Actually, the task isn't as difficult as it might seem. So few companies consistently and effectively market themselves that your investment will pay off with big results.

16

Many companies rely on useless, half-hearted, unimaginative, and lackluster marketing efforts. Some may even have marketing departments—at least that's the name on the door. But, when it comes right down to it, they have an outstanding track record for systematically and efficiently wasting just about every dollar they commit to their marketing efforts. Here are seven ways that they do just that:

1. *They shoot from the hip.* This is what we might call the world's most common marketing "plan." Of course, it's no plan at all. Even so, many otherwise sophisticated businesses believe they are marketing their products or services effectively by doing a mailing now, a couple of ads twice a year, and a brochure somewhere in between. "Do we have a newsletter to keep our customers informed? Darn tootin'. Hey, Tom. When was the last time we published it? (pause) Was it really five years ago?"

   Oh, from time to time, they revise the price sheet or think about correcting the phone number on the brochure. But such activities do not add up to a plan, an understanding, an organization, a purpose—or any results. Marketing demands a carefully conceived plan. Of course, changes will have to be made to the plan. But, if you don't know what you want to accomplish, the plan will never go anywhere.

2. *They take action only when they need to beef up sales.* Too many companies are guilty of spending their marketing dollars only when sales lag. This is the time when someone finds enough money to sign up for a trade show or get out a mailing. They don't know what's going to happen at the show or what should be said in the direct mail program. Usually, before any of that ever happens, the emergency passes and marketing goes back on the shelf until the next crisis rears its ugly head.

17

3. *They make their secretary the marketing director.* "Who's in charge of marketing around here?" Don't panic, everything is in good hands—the sales manager's secretary is the "Marketing Director." She orders pamphlets and letterhead. And when the company needed a brochure, she contracted with a friend who was actually a forklift operator but really liked to do art work. He did the whole job for fifty bucks. Sound exaggerated? The details vary, but this kind of delegation happens every day at companies in all parts of the country. For these firms, marketing is just a way to do brochures, mailings, and printing, and not what marketing is actually all about—getting customers!

4. *They duplicate what their competition is doing.* When it comes to marketing, some firms rival the CIA in terms of espionage. They know exactly what the competition is doing almost before it happens. When Proctor & Gamble introduced its Duncan Hines cookies, for example, it claimed a Keebler employee had taken aerial photos of its unfinished cookie factory, that a Frito Lay employee had infiltrated a secret P&G meeting, and that a Nabisco employee had wormed his way into a top secret area of P&G's processing plant.

   At other companies, rival employees have posed as utility and telephone workers to gain access to restricted areas. They've even been known to pay janitorial staff for trash from the executive suite. These shrewd 007 maneuvers go a long way towards building a customer base, right?

   Even for companies that wouldn't even think of engaging in corporate espionage, there is another strange fascination with competition. "If a competitor does it, then we should do it"—without even asking if what the competition is doing is really effective. Playing "copycat" is not just for kids. Companies do it all the time.

5. *They plan on a miracle.* Many people have an incredible mind-set when it comes to marketing. They send out a mailing and expect to get at least a 25 percent response! There is no consideration given to the content of the mailing, the quality of the list, or the needs of the customers or prospects. Doing it is all that's necessary.

   Similarly, they believe that if they spend ten thousand dollars, then there should be $100,000 in sales. In fact, many demand a certain multiple of the ad cost to justify further insertions. A Shearson Lehman Hutton sales manager once told us, "If we spend $5,000 in advertising, we must get back $50,000 in fees." Not sales, but commissions! That's how the magic thinking goes (When *we* talk, *everyone* listens!). Of course, there's rarely a miracle and someone inevitably comments, "See, marketing doesn't work. Just get sales to work a little harder. That's all we need."

6. *They ignore research.* "We know what we need," says the company's macho marketing mogul. "We've got the best product at the right price. All we need to do is tell people about it." That's right. Who needs research on prospective customers—how they think, their buying patterns, and their problems? "Don't worry. Just ask our sales guys. They have everything we need to know." So, big bucks are spent on classy brochures, self-mailers, and countless flyers. They look great but they don't produce results—and most of them are still sitting in the storeroom gathering dust.

7. *They avoid quality printing and design.* If you look like a bum, you may be one. Appearances may be deceiving, but they are also revealing. If your marketing materials

look like the junk mail sitting in the bottom of your trash barrel, you have no respect for your product, your company—or your prospects. If you have a good story, then dignify it with a quality presentation.

There's nothing magic about these ways of making certain you throw away your marketing budget. Which is why you should make every effort to avoid them. Marketing is too important to be sidetracked or derailed by the kind of ignorance that abounds in many firms today. It is the only way of getting and keeping customers, so the money needed to make marketing happen should never be squandered.

MARKETING BLUNDERS OF THE PROS

So far, we've been addressing companies that either ignore marketing altogether or pay it lip service. What about those businesses staffed with professional marketeers? Even though they may have sophisticated marketing operations, they often make a common mistake. We call it "Pride of Position."

Pride of Position is simply believing you are looking at marketing—and the marketplace—from the customers' viewpoint, while in fact you are operating from very carefully contrived personal prejudices. In other words, you recreate reality to guarantee your own personal and corporate comfort and security.

The Pride of Position problem afflicts just about every business, regardless of its size or industry. Take Sears, the giant retailer. Early in 1989, Sears announced a new "revolutionary" marketing strategy. In order to compete effectively with the discounters, every day would be sale day at Sears. Millions and millions of dollars were spent convincing consumers that prices had been slashed permanently on 50,000 items in the Sears stores.

How did this brilliant change come about? Perhaps someone at Sears developed the profound insight that discounting was the wave of the future and that this is what the customers want. So, the only way to make the point stick was to go all the way with discounting. What would be good for Sears would, of course, be good for the customer.

Evidently, no one at Sears bothered to consider the long-term implications of the "every day is sale day" approach. As a result, sales figures rose amid the initial media blitz. Spend a fortune in a short period and something will happen. And indeed something did! Wanting to see what all the hoopla was about, the crowds came. Then, as quickly as they arrived, the customers faded away when the big advertising dollars disappeared. As soon as the ads stopped running, the customers stopped buying. What was a sale yesterday and the day before is strictly ho-hum today.

Sears's solution was more Pride of Position thinking—"super sales," with new low, *low* prices! "But, wait a minute," says the consumer. "We thought *every* day was sale day at Sears." All this has put Sears on a path of endless sales, even lower prices, and incredible confusion in the minds of consumers. The end of the road, though, might be a going-out-of-business sale. (Remember another great retailer that tried this technique—Korvettes. Its chain of discount stores went the same route—straight into oblivion.)

Within nine months after announcing its revolutionary new marketing program, the Sears Tower in Chicago, the world's tallest building, was up for sale. Total embarrassment was avoided for this grand old company when someone came along and refinanced the real estate that is perhaps the world's tallest symbol of Pride of Position.

Interestingly, Sears officials now realize that differentiation is the name of the marketing game in retailing and they are returning to their solid long-standing "satisfaction guaranteed" marketing tradition. They've evidently learned that trying to manipulate customers is nothing other than ill-founded arrogance. This viewpoint only ends in disaster, because customer confidence is what marketing is all about. To betray that confidence by thinking it is permissible to play games with the buying public is to drive customers straight into the arms of the competition. What customers really want and need is credibility from a company.

A lack of customer understanding is found in other businesses and industries, too. We once talked to a Merrill Lynch broker who had made a cold call to us and proudly reported that his firm had trained him in "consultative selling." This is evidently an attempt by the brokerage house to differentiate its sales personnel from thousands of other brokers who go for the jugular over the phone. To Merrill Lynch's credit, the firm recognizes that it must separate itself from the competition.

All this is well and good, but it is also total nonsense from a marketing perspective. What management decides to do—in this case make its sales reps look different by making them so-called "consultative salespeople"—is irrelevant. Why? Because the person who gets the call from the Merrill Lynch rep can't distinguish this highly trained, competent "consultative salesperson" from everyone else representing a brokerage firm. Just changing the words doesn't do the job.

So, the Merrill Lynch executives (and anyone else, of course) can sit in their planning meetings and dream up new and clever techniques. But they completely miss the real problem by practicing Pride of Position thinking. The simple truth of the matter is that you can't expect to be successful if you ignore the marketplace. What Merrill Lynch (or anyone else) thinks isn't important. How their sales reps are perceived by the customer is all that counts.

As you can see, even companies that understand the importance of marketing often fail to do it well. That's because they subscribe to the "geocentric myth," which states that the world revolves around their own corporate headquarters. Of course, the world really revolves around their customers' headquarters. If you believe this is heresy, then you might as well close this book—you're probably happy with your current level of sales, profits, and performance. If, however, you want to learn how to cultivate customers and create a buying environment that will carry you through the good times and tough times alike, read on. You might even come to believe, as Willy Loman so eloquently put it, that selling truly is the "greatest career a man could want." All you need is the right marketing support.

Chapter
THREE

———— ✧ ————

Selling in the 1990s

Introduction to
Magnet Marketing

Graham's Law: Techniques don't make sales.

NEW ANSWERS TO AN OLD QUESTION

Ask 100 people, "Why is your company in business?" and they'll inevitably answer, "To survive, grow, and make a profit." Ask 100 salespeople the same question and you'll get the same answer. Ask 100 business school students and professors for their opinion, and you'll again hear survival... growth...and profitability.

Of course, every business must survive, grow, and profit if it is to succeed. But long-term success results from a more fundamental activity: creating customers. If you believe that the primary responsibility of your company is to create customers, then staying in business, growing, and making a profit cease to become issues, because you'll have a continual supply of customers who want to do business with you. You'll also be practicing "magnet marketing," a philosophy devoted to the cultivation of customers.

Magnet marketing is based on the idea that when you properly cultivate customers, they'll be naturally attracted to your company. It recognizes that by building solid relationships with customers, you'll become their vendor of choice. It also recognizes that to succeed in the cultivation process, you must build a bridge with customers and prospects that enables you to be in the right place at the right time. Magnet marketing solves the timing problem by getting the customer to come to you rather than chasing them for a sale. In doing so, it allows salespeople to follow up on leads and do what is expected of them—make sales.

In addition, magnet marketing pulls everyone in the company together and aligns their efforts along the same pole. Marketing people pave the way for customer orders, salespeople close the deal when customers are ready to buy, and the manufacturing or service arms of the company give customers the most for their dollar. When this happens, the whole effort is greater than the sum of the parts. The momentum from each sale motivates everyone in the company to find new ways of creating customers and holding their business for the long term.

Is this desirable state of affairs achieved through new tricks? No. In fact, magnet marketing draws on conventional tools of the trade—advertising, newsletters, direct mail, and so on. It just uses them in new ways.

Consider the case of Ed Testa, an account executive at Graphics Leasing Corp. Testa admits that for several years his sales were far below his colleagues'. Now all that has changed. Today he's straight out. His desk is covered with pending deals and his phone rings off the hook. Why? Because Ed became a magnet marketeer. Every time he took a business trip he copied pages from the phone book and stayed in touch with people in his area. And he spent most of his time getting acquainted and answering questions, rather than pushing for sales. Ed made sure that everyone he had contacted went onto his mailing list and received the company's *SalesMaker Bulletin* newsletter, which contained invaluable tips for client companies.

In short, Ed got his priorities straight. Even though he's a salesman, he knows that in his company he must also wear a marketing hat in order to create an environment in which people will want to do business with him—now, next month, or a year from now. "The small deals have grown into big ones," he reports. "A lot of my new business comes from word-of-mouth, as well as repeat orders from my existing customers." Wisely, Ed continues to add prospects to his list and keep in touch on a regular basis through notes and the newsletter.

As Ed discovered, magnet marketing turns the tables by reversing the usual "sales and marketing" process. It keeps the priorities straight by placing the emphasis on identifying and cultivating prospects, generating new leads, and building customer loyalty to the company.

While magnet marketing involves conventional tools of the trade, it integrates them into a larger philosophy of customer cultivation. When companies think about customer cultivation, they change their internal focus from "What can we do to our salespeople to make them more effective?" to "What can we do to the customers to get them to buy from us?"

Customers will be naturally attracted to your company if you deploy your marketing resources and salespeople in the right way. This is achieved by exercising the following three principles:

1. Think long term.

2. Get the customer to want you.

3. Be there when customer gets ready to buy.

In the following sections, we'll discuss the key magnet marketing techniques related to each principle. We'll also list "award" winners from Graham's Hall of Magnet Marketing Fame, companies that have done an exemplary job of mastering customer cultivation principles and techniques.

THINK LONG TERM

The curse of business is that most companies think for today. They face crisis after crisis and respond with the same fire-fighting mentality: "Let's have a sale!" "Let's 'kick butt' and get our salesforce out there—raise the quotas!" And so on. We've all heard of, or have been subjected to, this Cro-Magnon approach to making things happen. Of course, nothing happens, because no one develops a lasting solution to the core problems.

Part of the problem arises from the intense pressures placed on managers to hit the desired fiscal "bogey." But if your thinking extends only as far as the next quarter profits, then you're pushing product or services, not creating customers. And as we'll demonstrate again and again throughout this book, the ability to create customers is the only long-term guarantee of sustained sales.

While there's nothing wrong with an occasional short-term promotion to take advantage of seasonal opportunities or clear out inventories, such flash-in-the pan tactics must not eclipse long-term thinking. In Chapter 2, we saw how the "every day is sale day" mentality painted Sears into a tight corner. Other companies, too, are floundering in a self-generated sea of gimmicks and hype. They simply don't realize that contests, prizes, and the like are just pressure-cooker schemes that mask the absence of conditions conducive to buying. Moreover, companies that sponsor occasional gimmicks don't understand that what counts in marketing is the *cumulative* effect of many individual techniques. Bouncing one ball in the air doesn't attract any great interest. Juggling a half dozen balls creates a magnetic effect that captures the interest of customers.

A magnet marketing program is an *investment* in the future. While the individual components—a particular ad, a customer newsletter, or a series of customer education articles—may not foster immediate results, over time the integrated strategy will pay off.

Consider the multifaceted marketing campaign that Credit Data of New England took. When this company retained us in 1983, its client list consisted of 165 members. We suggested a mix of newsletters, direct mail, and print ads, as well as special events such as an annual golf tournament, with the proceeds being donated to worthy causes. We also suggested that the company produce an annual report—even though legally none was required for this type of business. The candor of the reporting, we felt, would boost this firms credibility.

During the first six months, the client level remained the same. But 18 months later, the list had grown to 854! (which represents a 120 percent increase in revenues). This company deferred its "profit gratification," patiently waiting for the seeds of its efforts to sprout. And the results were more than worth the delay.

Many other companies are to be commended for their long-term views, too. Here are two winners from Graham's Hall of Fame:

1. WordPerfect Corporation wins an award for maintaining the undisputed best customer support service in the PC software industry. The company spends about $500,000 a month on its toll-free line, and maintains a stable of 600 technical support people, each of whom is extremely knowledgeable. If they don't know the answer to your problem, they'll promptly research it and call you back. Even though WordPerfect owns 60 percent of the PC word processing market, the company knows that to maintain its needs, it can never rest on its laurels. Now *that's* long-term thinking in action.

2. The IRS deserves an honorable mention for realizing that it can win more taxpayers with honey than with a stick. Since 1988, when the U.S. Congress passed the Taxpayers Bill of Rights, the Service has bent over backwards to ensure that its representatives are courteous and friendly. Supervisors randomly monitor telephone inquiries to ensure that taxpayers are treated well and receive accurate information. While no one likes paying taxes, the IRS has gone a long way to ensure more cooperation from its "customers."

GET THE CUSTOMER TO WANT *YOU*

To make more sales, your customers must possess a positive predisposition towards your products or services. One of the major tasks of any company is to educate the prospective customers (this topic is discussed in depth in Chapter 8). In fact, what sets one company apart from others is the degree to which it translates its expertise, knowledge, and experience

31

into helpful and timely information and assistance for its customers and prospects. Companies that understand the importance of education stand out as solid, capable, and stable.

Inevitably, good customer education emerges into effective, continuous customer cultivation. It becomes a process of helping people to believe in and trust you long before any move takes place to make a sale. In this way, customer education eventually draws the prospect to you.

Despite these benefits, the idea of education seems to produce a negative response from many salespeople. Sales managers want "results," so anything that takes time is viewed as irrelevant to the selling process. That's a big mistake. In fact, it may be the biggest error of all. Without proper education, there is no way to increase sales.

The company's "educational" or marketing program should be aimed at having the customer come to one conclusion: "This is what I want and this is the firm I am going to buy it from." Whether you do it through newsletters, technical bulletins, newspaper/magazine articles, or seminars, show customers that your prime interest is helping them improve their well-being, profits, or happiness in some way. When customers believe that you're motivated by fulfilling their needs rather than lining your own pockets, you automatically become...the vendor of choice! Why buy from anyone else?

Also, bringing your company's expertise and experience to bear on problems faced by customers serves to elevate you in the eyes of both customers and prospects. Your firm is seen in a new and different light. Instead of being regarded just as a "vendor," you're seen as a supplier of information. This changes the sales situation dramatically. The buyer wants what your company has to offer—demonstrated knowledge and experience. It is no longer a matter of furnishing references or trying to persuade through a self-serving proposal. "Bells and whistles" cease to be an issue; the goods or services are only a means to an end, not the focal point of the sale.

The following companies receive high marks in Graham's Hall of Magnet Marketing Fame for their customer education efforts:

1. DAK Industries Incorporated wins a first place award for its brilliant use of customer education as a marketing tool. Each DAK catalog contains 70 to 100 items selected from among thousands as being exceptional in terms of value and performance. Like other up-scale "high-tech toy catalogs," DAK provides a wealth of valuable information about each item—what problems it will solve for you, how it works, and what benefits you'll derive buy owning one, among other topics. The DAK catalog also includes supplementary articles that describe a particular technology. Equally important, DAK issues its catalog on a quarterly basis. So even if you're not ready to buy today, you know they'll be there tomorrow, ready to take your order.

   The Winter 1989 DAK catalog, for example, devotes nine pages to the explanation of how radar detectors work (that's 10 percent of the entire catalog). The article is clearly written and presents solid information. Even those who aren't in the market for radar detectors, but are curious as to how the things work, will likely glance at it. If at some point they do become interested in buying a detector, guess where they'll turn to?

   For those who are actively seeking radar detection devices, the article gives them the information they need to make an informed buying decision. And it will most likely center around one of the detectors offered in the catalog. Well done, DAK!

2. Wassau Insurance wins an award for creating the image that Wassau *means* business. While most insurance companies' advertisements present a nebulous "feel

good" strategy, Wassau focuses relentlessly on being the vendor of choice for businesses.

3. Tupperware has earned an honorable mention for pioneering the Tupperware parties, in which homemakers learn about what to do with the company's various plastic containers. Through the educational process, party attendees learn valuable tips for the kitchen—and place orders for armloads of the company's products.

BE THERE WHEN CUSTOMER GETS READY TO BUY

Sales aren't lost because of a lack of aggressive salesmanship, but because the salesperson isn't there when the customer is ready to place an order. Whether a company sells a product or service, its primary responsibility is to ensure that a buying environment exists when the customer is ready to buy. Obviously, salespeople can't be everywhere all the time. That's why you need a magnet marketing strategy that pulls customers to you. This is not to suggest that the salesperson becomes little more than an order taker; to the contrary, the salesperson is a major player in the customer cultivation process. But it does mean that the company representative enters the sales situation with the customer in a buying frame of mind.

It is easy to spot a company with a buying environment because it will have outstanding credibility with its customers. When the salesperson walks through the door, the customer already possesses an image of the company itself. Whether it is through advertising, direct mail, articles in the media, or a combination of all of these, the company has launched a program to create a simple message in the customer's mind: this particular firm is the one to buy from.

Even though this may seem somewhat fundamental, most businesses leave it to the salesperson to "sell" the customer on the company. Listen to the next salesperson who comes through your door. Inevitably, the sales pitch will begin with an attempt to establish the company's credibility—"we're the oldest, the largest, the leader," and so forth. To give the salesperson this task is like hanging a huge rock around a swimmer's neck, and then expecting him to compete successfully in a race. Long before the salesperson arrives on the scene, the prospect must have made a conscious decision to do business with your firm.

PC's Ltd. is an excellent example of a company that recognizes the value of building credibility with the customer. PC's Ltd. created the first mail order alternative to IBM and Compaq and stunned the world with the fastest and smallest desktop computer on the market. In review after review, PC's Ltd. won kudos for technical innovation and reliability. To further its reputation and grab more market share from Big Blue and the other top tier computer makers, PC's Ltd. sought and found a massive cash infusion, enabling it to build state-of-the-art manufacturing plants and hire the best engineers in the business.

When the retooling was complete, the company, now called Dell Computers, after its maverick founder, Michael Dell, ran full-page ads in the major computer magazines showing people the new facilities and the new wares. Its brochures focused as much on the new company as the new products, showing people that Dell was indeed a major player in the PC field. By spending the time, energy, and money to establish itself as the leading IBM/Compaq alternative, Dell has fostered a buying environment that is naturally attracting a greater share of PC customers each year.

Here are a few other commendable entries in Graham's Hall of Magnet Marketing Fame:

1. Federal Express. When it absolutely, positively has to be there overnight, who's the vendor of choice? For a good portion of the world, it's Fed X. Through its advertising campaigns, Federal Express has made itself the *de facto* standard of overnight delivery. In many

parts of the country, the name "Fed X" has become synonymous with fast overnight delivery, just as Kleenex is now used generically for "tissue" and Xerox for "photocopying."

Federal Express is also to be commended for delivering on its promises, having invested in the most sophisticated package tracking system of any of the courier companies. Customers can call at any hour of the day and generally within a few minutes learn the disposition of their package. In addition, Federal Express arms its users with a wide assortment of customizable free shipping materials, making it easy for any company of any size to quickly assemble a package at the last moment.

Given its technological sophistication, cheery operators and delivery personnel, and outstanding track record, Fed X is to be congratulated for creating a solid buying environment.

2. When you're ready to buy a camcorder, who do you think of? Sony. When you think of small color TVs, who do you think of? Sony. When you think of personal hand-held music systems, who do you think of? Sony.

   Through its ad campaigns and distribution strategies, Sony establishes itself as the market leader in whatever sectors it breaks new ground (Betamax being a rare flop for the company). As a result, the name Sony conjures up images of the best in personal electronic audio/visual devices. With its vast network of dealers and rich product lines, Sony is there when customers are ready to buy.

3. American Express deserves an honorable mention for pioneering the quarterly and annual expense management reports. American Express expanded the function of the credit card industry by providing its card users

with useful information about their expenditures. The reports make it easy for assembling personal tax information and reporting business expenses. The message is loud and clear: when you want a credit card for business travel, AMEX is the vendor of choice.

THE RESULTS OF MAGNET MARKETING

When the three principles of magnet marketing are translated into action plans, everything else falls into place. Sales levels usually soar, because customers feel driven to buy from the company. Salespeople no longer have to guess when customers are ready to buy, so they don't waste time with cold calls or canvassing. As marketing people generate leads, the sales force easily closes the deals.

Magnet marketing also has dramatic effects on the company's stability. Salespeople stop complaining about not having enough leads, about problems with name or product recognition, and about lost sales due to "high prices." The turnover rate plummets and the company becomes the employer of choice.

As the company builds and fortifies a buying environment with its customers, it enjoys two other benefits. Firstly, the customers keep coming back, regardless of changes in the marketplace and the economy. With a stable flow of orders, the company doesn't have to think of itself as a cork tossed about a stormy sea. Deals are closed and sales are made on the strength of the company's products and services, not external factors.

Secondly, customers attracted by magnet marketing tend to stick. In fact, they're so enamored with the company that they become immune to the overtures of competitors. These are the customers who give you the benefit of the doubt when a problem arises. This loyalty factor becomes the cornerstone of a strong and effective competitive position (see Chapter 9 for a complete discussion of how magnet marketing generates repeat business).

So far we've cited large corporations to illustrate how magnet marketing gets results. Below we show how the same techniques can be applied to small (even one-person operations) and medium-size firms as well.

After 20 years of serving as the human resources manager for a major corporation, John Morgan decided to strike out on his own as a personnel consultant. For the first three years, John did business with his old employers. Business was so good, he felt no need to seek new clients. But a series of shake-ups at his various alma maters left him high and dry. John frantically began making cold calls to drum up new business, but found the going slow. "None of these people know me," he comments. "Unlike my original clients, these new voices on the phone don't have the faintest idea who I am or what I can do."

Morgan then realized it was time to stop wasting his energy cold calling and start doing something that would have a "natural client pull." So he began writing articles for trade magazines and business publications, offering insights and tips that companies could put to immediate use. The result? Within six months, Morgan had to turn away clients who begged for his advice.

Federal Heating & Engineering Co., Inc., a well-established home heating oil dealer north of Boston, was faced with tough competition from "discounters" cutting prices as much as 20 cents a gallon on the one hand, and from the bigger players offering 200 gallons of free oil, television sets, microwave ovens, and other giveaways to new customers. Federal Heating's president and founder, Al LaPointe, knew the pitfalls of giving away the store. "We'd be out of business in three years," he commented to us.

How could Federal Heating maintain its position in the marketplace with price wars and giveaway programs raging all around it? By rewriting the rules of the game. Instead of dropping to its knees, the company began mailing a snazzy newsletter featuring stories about local personalities, helpful information on ways to reduce energy costs, and other high-interest tidbits to more than 25,000 area residents using fuel oil. The right mix of information and entertainment made the newsletter an instant hit, which not only gave the company high visibility with prospects, but also created a sense of pride among its customers. The regular newsletter helps insulate customers from price attacks by Federal's competitors.

Today, Federal Heating continues to win the war for market share without firing a shot at its competition; instead, it has funneled resources and energy into a vehicle that attracts prospects and keeps customers.

Michael Kenealy, founder of Key Realty, knew he could develop a highly successful commercial real estate firm by staking out a limited territory in a large East Coast city. And he was right—within two years after opening its doors, Key Realty was handling by far the majority of commercial deals in the area. That is, until some of the large regional firms rode into town with their bloated marketing budgets and tantalizing sales pitches. At that point, Kenealy and his staff felt the pinch. Deals that normally came to him slipped into the hands of the new players.

To fight back, Kenealy decided to become the expert on every piece of commercial and industrial property in the city. So he hired a programmer to develop a sophisticated database containing everything known on available properties. He then conducted a well-targeted direct mail and advertising campaign, announcing his new capabilities. His PR agent also arranged for a major news feature on Key Realty's unique database.

Before long, anyone who wanted to know about a particular property thought about Kenealy's operation, since no one else had the kind of detailed, accurate information that sat in Key Reality's computer. It became obvious that this company had the knowledge to put deals together, while the cash-rich, but information-poor, competitors had nothing but slippery smooth sales pitches and glitzy brochures. As a result of Kenealy's efforts, Key Realty has leased and sold more square feet in the city than any other commercial reality outfit in the area.

In each of the cases, magnet marketing enabled a business to become the vendors of choice and leave its competition in the dust. In the first case, the oil company attracted customers by providing free educational information through its newsletter and by making a consistent impact on both customers and prospects. The company demonstrated that it had a long term interest in its customers' well being, giving it an edge despite its higher prices.

In the second situation, the consultant also conveyed valuable information by writing articles that caught the eyes of potential clients and drew them to the phone...like a magnet!

Finally, the commercial real estate firm took another tact with magnet marketing. It became the expert on its product—property. Because the company had armed itself with pertinent knowledge, clients beat a path to the door.

As you can see, magnet marketing dramatizes a company's message by establishing a highly focused point of view. The magnet marketeer pounds away at what can be called "the company theme," which projects the firm as innovative and on the cutting edge. Magnet marketing finely tunes your message so that it gets through with clarity and impact to the type of customer with whom you want to do business.

Whether it is through the consistent use of customer oriented newsletters, information articles published in business and trade journals, surveys, special reports, news stories, advertising, or seminars, magnet marketing singles out your company as the vendor of choice. It gives your company high visibility *all the time*, which is essential to establishing a strong leadership position.

In addition, taking a magnet marketing approach sets your priorities straight. When you see your primary job as creating customers, you'll find yourself awash in prospect leads and customer allegiance. The sales staff won't be out on the street trying to find customers like needles in a haystack. They won't be spending valuable time trying to convince prospects to buy. Rather, they'll be out every day doing their job—continuing the cultivation process *and* making sales from people who want to do business with your company.

Of course, magnet marketing is not a substitute for poor products or inadequate service. But it does put a company in charge of its destiny, enabling it to look down the road with confidence because the pipeline is constantly replenished with new prospects. The ups and downs disappear. Salespeople stick around and the entire company gets invigorated because the marketplace perceives your firm to be upbeat and positive.

Will magnet marketing work for you? That depends on whether or not you're willing to make a serious commitment of time and energy towards building long-term profitability. In the following chapters, you'll find a complete program for developing your own integrated approach to magnet marketing. It consists of a conceptual framework, as well as specific techniques that you can mold to your company's products or services.

Before diving into the program, bear in mind one final point: Magnet marketing is a company-wide effort, not just the isolated responsibility of your marketing and sales departments. For magnet marketing to work, everyone must pull together and make a commitment to making the company the vendor of choice, to creating the right buying environment, and to delivering the goods and services that customers are expecting to purchase. Total customer loyalty requires total quality—at all levels of the company.

———— ✧ ————

Taking Stock

How to Assess Your Marketing Effectiveness and Develop Customer Cultivation Goals

*Graham's Law: If you're not growing
prospects today, you won't have any
customers tomorrow.*

LOOKING INWARD

Common sense dictates that a company should evaluate its marketing program regularly. This is often easier said than done, though. The day-to-day pressures of selling, coping with customers, and solving basic business problems make it difficult to do a marketing appraisal.

As a result, most firms only look at their marketing effectiveness when a crisis arises. An upstart competitor suddenly appears on the scene with loss-leader pricing. Another competitor introduces a breakthrough product that renders yours obsolete. A rise in interest rates pulls the rug out from under your industry. These are the kinds of events that force companies to evaluate their strengths and weaknesses. After all, it may be a matter of life and death.

Even when a company does have occasion to evaluate its marketing program, though, it often has a difficult time being objective. That's why it's critical to have a basic set of guidelines for judging a company's marketing program. The following "red flags" are meant to help you identify hidden weak spots in your marketing program. Rather than providing quantitative measures, such as, "if your marketing budget is only 1.34 percent of your total operating budget, then you should do X, Y, and Z," the flags give you a general sense of what's wrong with your marketing approach. The fact that you're only spending 1.34 percent of your operating funds on marketing is a *symptom* of a larger issue. In fact, it can be the result of any of the problems described on the following pages.

As you read through the chapter, ask yourself if we are describing *your* company. If you can identify with any of the issues we raise, your company needs to review and make some serious changes in its marketing plan. The good news is that in the next chapters you'll find everything you need to make the necessary changes happen in your business. And by identifying your areas of weakness now, you'll be able to focus on the tips and techniques that can help your company get back on track and compete at the highest possible level. Now spend a few minutes to take the pulse of your company's marketing efforts.

Five Signs of an Ailing Marketing Program

1. *Price is the driving force.* If having "the lowest price" is your primary way of keeping and attracting customers, then you have a very serious marketing problem. Deep discounts, special concessions, and eternal "specials" (like "every day is sale day" at Sears—see Chapter 2) are sure signs of trouble.

   The "lowest price" approach keeps you on the run because customers see you only as a means of getting something. When that happens, you're merely a conduit for goods or services. Unfortunately, many businesses actually see themselves this way—a cog in the distribution system. These companies can't get a fair price because they are not cultivating the perception of value in the minds of their customers. Ultimately, this will spell disaster.

2. *Frequent changes in sales strategies.* This month it's a contest. Next month it's win a trip to the Falkland Islands. Then, it's a "special bonus." Pick up an idea here or there, and the next morning the idea has become this week's "sales program!"

   Oddly, companies that adopt the "Floating Crap Game Strategy" often consider themselves "sales driven"—if everyone just pushed a little harder, they could meet their goals. In reality, the "strategy" amounts to little more than a collection of desperate moves. Without a unified plan, the company cannot hope to communicate a unified message that cultivates customers. Only a well-designed marketing program can provide the magnetism needed to attract and keep a solid customer base.

3. *Most leads come from the sales staff.* Of course, salespeople should develop leads. But if this is the primary way a company attracts new business, then there's a major flaw in the marketing program. A solid marketing program should yield a constant flow of new business leads. Throwing more and more salespeople out in the field is both expensive and inefficient if the objective is "go get more business." Even the best salesperson cannot always be at the right place at the right time. Only a well-developed marketing program can make the company's presence felt when the customer or prospect is ready to buy. Without a strong marketing program in place, salespeople will spend most of their energy spinning their wheels.

4. *Your customers often say, "I didn't know you carried that."* If you hear this type of comment from your customers, then you can be certain your company is doing a poor job of educating its customers. Few companies actually maximize the sales potential in their existing customer base, let alone continually attract new customers. This happens because the marketing program isn't designed to keep customers and prospects properly informed. Without a constant stream of information, customers will simply assume that you cannot fulfill their needs and will seek other vendors who can.

5. *Your mailing list is inadequate.* A company's mailing list may be the single most important way to evaluate its marketing program. Although it seems easy, few companies can produce a complete, up-to-date, accessible list. Sure, most firms have a customer list, but many of the entries lack an individual's name. Mail is sent to "CEO", or "Vice President of Sales," or "Purchasing

Manager." That means the CEO doesn't know you. The Vice President of Sales doesn't know you. And the Purchasing Manager doesn't know you. In fact, the only people who know that you exist may be the secretary who processes your invoices or the janitor who incinerates your junk mail.

What about your prospects? Are your salespeople adding new names? Is the mailing list updated on a regular basis? If you wanted to send a personal letter to everyone in a particular territory, could you do it—automatically?

If you have difficulty answering these questions, you can be sure your company is not staying in close touch with its most valuable resource—customers and prospects. Should it be surprising that not enough people know you? Should you be distressed because so few leads are coming through the door? Absolutely not—because without an effective marketing program, there's no reason they should.

Most companies will admit to at least one of these signs of marketing weakness, even those that have been in business for decades. Even the slightest impairment in marketing functions means that they are not communicating as efficiently and effectively with customers and prospects as they could. Unless they adopt a strong marketing orientation, they will either remain "stuck" at their present level or slowly lose ground until they are no longer competitive.

Now that you know some of your marketing frailties, let's turn to the positive side of the spectrum and answer the question: Where do you want to be in six months?, ...in one year?, ...in five years?, and so on. We're not talking about numerical goals—"We want to own 33.4 percent of the foot deodorant market" or "We want to see consistent annual growth of 21.6 percent"—but marketing effectiveness goals—"We want to be able to attract customers even during economic downturns,"

"We want our customers to think of us as problem solvers, not just mere suppliers," and so on. The following section provides 12 generic goals that any company can achieve once it commits itself to a magnet marketing program.

DECIDE TO BECOME MARKETING-DRIVEN

Earlier, we hinted at the difference between sales-driven and marketing-driven companies. Now let's probe a little deeper into why companies that adopt a marketing-driven position are so much stronger and more competitive. If the focus is on sales, then the product or service is all important. But if the company focuses on what the customer (and prospect) needs and wants, marketing becomes an overriding concern.

A company's long-term success is best served by assuming a marketing-driven posture. Why? Because the role of marketing is to create the right conditions for sales to take place. Marketers ask the questions, "What does the customer want?" "What does the customer expect?" What are the conditions we need to create so the customer wants to do business with us?" In other words, marketing makes sales easier. Companies that do become marketing-driven enjoy a wealth of benefits, the most common of which are presented below.

As you read through the list of benefits, visualize your company in six months or a year. Imagine what it would be like to be a salesperson for your revitalized firm. Imagine what customers would be saying about your products and services. And imagine the kind of positive press that your company would enjoy as a result of its high level of customer responsiveness.

This is far more than wishful thinking. Athletes use this kind of "guided imagery" to help them achieve extraordinary feats. Critically ill people use it to conquer seemingly incurable diseases. And business people can use it to orient their thoughts and actions along the path to success. You, too, can use the following marketing benefits to mentally paint your company in broad brush strokes. Then, as you read the next chapters, you can begin filling in the fine details, which will help you translate your dreams into reality.

If you're company is in it for the long haul, make it a priority to become marketing-driven. A magnet marketing program dedicated to customer cultivation will enable you to do just that. In the next chapters, you'll learn about the three core tools of a magnet marketing program: self-promotion, media relations, and advertising. When combined in the right proportions, these customer cultivation tools will help you reactivate former customers, increase business with current customers, and convert prospects who otherwise might turn to your competitors.

The company that cultivates well is like a patient hunter; after planting the bait, it lies ready and waiting for the customer to return for more. The smart cultivators know just when to make their move. After all, it makes more sense to meet with prospects when they actually want to buy than to make a cold call and try to convince them they need your product or service. Like birth and death, every sale happens when it's supposed to happen. If the cultivation process has gone well, the prospect will seek out the company as the vendor of choice.

HOW TO BECOME MARKETING-DRIVEN
Designing Your Own Magnet Marketing Program

In order for a marketing plan to accomplish anything significant, it must be workable. And, it must be simple and clear so that it will capture the imagination and support of management. In other words, it must make immediate sense!

To launch magnet marketing in your company, we recommend what we call the "On Your Mark, Get Set, Go" program. Here's what it entails:

On Your Mark

The first step is to define your magnet marketing objectives for a particular period of time, most likely the next 12 months. What is it you want to accomplish? Here are some typical goals:

1. *Establish your firm as a permanent player.* You may know you are a solid business, but that's not nearly as important as how you are perceived by your customers, your prospects, and your competition. Successful marketing influences the perceptions of others. Good marketing allows you to shape the way other people think and, therefore, how they buy.

2. *Gain a competitive advantage.* Everyone wants a level playing field, although such a state of affairs represents an ideal that will never be achieved. It won't do you much good wishing that things will be different—that the Japanese didn't make cars, the Koreans weren't in electronics, and so on. Nothing can guarantee that the field will be totally level, but you *can* get partially rid of the hills and valleys through effective marketing. Good marketing gives you that extra head of steam to continue charging down the field, no matter what the opposing team throws at you, and no matter what surprises the economy has in store for you.

3. *Avoid a "crisis-to-crisis" business environment.* Many companies suffer through, rather than create, their futures. An effective marketing program will put you in control of your own destiny. You won't have to worry about being dependent on key accounts, because your magnet marketing tools will constantly draw a stream of fresh customers to your doorstep.

4. *Eliminate the need for "sales pushes."* How often do we hear a top manager say, "Well, let's get out there and get those sales up." You can't force sales any more than you

can speed up a sunrise. If your company is well known, respected, and trusted, sales come naturally. Companies that use magnet marketing expend their energy at a steady rate, which makes for a more productive, pleasant, and profitable operation.

5. *Focus on the customer.* A solid marketing program enables you to cultivate customers over a period of time. It allows you to show customers that you care about their business, and that you're playing for the long term. Remember, it's not what you want to sell that counts—the name of the game is recognizing *what the customer wants to buy*. And you'll only learn that through the cultivation process.

6. *Build enduring relationships with customers.* Today's customers are extremely sophisticated. They know when you are simply trying to clinch a sale and when you're adding genuine value. A good marketing program will enable your salespeople to be perceived more like consultants, as experts working with customers to help them achieve their goals.

7. *Gain control over your company's image.* In an age when we are bombarded with thousands and thousands of "messages" every waking hour, no one can afford to exhaustively analyze every potential supplier. So people tend to base their assessment on quick impressions. Right or wrong, they arrive at conclusions that stay with them. One of the primary functions of a marketing program should be to mold those impressions and make sure they telegraph the message you want to send.

8. *Retain customers.* Everyone loves new customers. But what about all those customers who are forgotten and just fade away? It is far more expensive to attract a new customer than it is to hold onto old ones. Marketing-

driven companies never lose sight of the *total* spectrum customers, from the "old faithfuls" to the prospects farthest on the fringe.

9. *Sell more to your present customers.* The greatest untapped source of increased sales is your present customer base. A primary function of marketing is to see to it that your customers are aware of everything you can do for them. As your capabilities, products, and services change and expand, you should be able to draw on your existing customer base. Marketing makes that happen.

10. *Attract the right customers.* If you're not seriously focusing on the customers you can best serve, then your business is not as productive as it should be. Magnet marketing allows you to place your resources where they'll do the most good.

11. *Spend your money wisely.* Marketing-driven companies achieve success by smoothly orchestrating many different actions into a seamless theme. And the total power of the theme is substantially greater than the sum of the parts.

12. *Devote your efforts to your real business.* What does a construction company do? Build buildings? No. It creates centers of profit for its clients. A building is only a means to an end. What does F.A.O. Schwartz sell? According to the company president, it's not toys. F.A.O. Schwartz sells fun. What about a marketing firm? What does it sell? Only one product—success!

If you're eager to get going, you can adopt all of the above goals. That's understandable, but it's also unrealistic to believe you can achieve all of them in one fell swoop. Work the list over and over until you are able to set forth three or four key objectives that will be the focus of your marketing program over the coming year.

That will be more than a handful!

Get Set

Now that you are "On Your Mark," you can move to the next step. You are ready to "Get Set." With your marketing objectives clearly in mind, the task is to build the activities that are required to meet these goals.

In working with our clients, we emphasize three types of marketing activities. Any effective marketing program must contain these elements: self-promotion, media relations, and advertising.

1. Self-promotion includes vehicles for telling your story to the world, such as newsletters, direct mail, seminars, and so on. How a newsletter fits into the marketing program, what it should contain, how often it should be published, and what it should look like are separate issues. The same is true for brochures and direct mail. In order for these activities to be successful—to assist in meeting the goals and objectives—requires special expertise. The basic issue, however, is to recognize that a company must engage in several self-promotional activities in order to have an effective marketing program (self-promotion is discussed at length in Chapter 5).

2. The second element in marketing is media relations. Quite often, we hear clients ask, "Who would want to write about us?" In fact, every company harbors a wealth of terrific news stories. A good media relations campaign will ferret out those stories and get the reporters and editors to come to you. It will also provide

the means for you to create your own press through "bylined articles." (Chapter 6 explains how to develop and profit from sound media relations.)

3. The third element of an effective marketing program is paid advertising. No marketing program is complete without an advertising component. To set the record straight, many people complain that advertising doesn't work. The fact is, the right ads, in the right place, over the right period of time make an impact. The major task in developing effective advertising is to make sure your ads reflect your marketing goals and objectives. When that happens, your advertising will produce for you. (See Chapter 7 for a discussion of how advertising fits into a magnet marketing program.)

If you take self-promotion, media relations, and advertising as 100 percent of the marketing pie, the degree to which each is emphasized depends on your objectives. The emphasis, however, need not be cast in stone and changes should be made as the need arises. The point is simply that a good marketing program demands that there be elements of all three woven together for maximum impact. Trying shortcuts won't work. Eliminating this or cutting back on that will only cause a program to fail. And, more often than not, this gives someone a reason to say, "You see, marketing doesn't work."

Go

The third and final step is to implement your program. To do so involves two questions: "What's the budget?" and "Who's going to do what to whom?" Or, as a colleague of ours says, "Who's going to make the coffee?"

What about the budget? How much should be spent on marketing? There are a number of possible answers, including a percentage of anticipated annual sales. Yet, the only true test of a marketing budget is this: Does it reflect your original goals and objectives? Remember, you can't reach the moon with a slingshot!

If you want to increase market share, it will require more money. If you want to maintain your presence in the marketplace, then the costs will be lower. What geography is involved: national, regional, local? This factor alone can influence a budget significantly.

Throughout the implementation or "Go" phase, the right people need to monitor all activities. Is everything on schedule? Are results being tracked? Are leads going to the sales department? What happens to them there? Do changes need to be made?

As time passes, a well-organized mailing list should be growing and growing. All past and present customers must be on the list. And a constant effort must be made to add prospects, since they're the future of your company. If you cannot push a button at any given moment and get a printout of your updated mailing list, you're in trouble.

Other vital issues in the "Go" stage include setting standards, maintaining objectivity, and staying on track. There's no substitute for high quality. It is essential to make certain what you do reflects the right image. Just getting something done is not good enough—strive to be the best.

The System Works

The "On Your Mark, Get Set, Go" program is designed to build an effective marketing program that meets today's needs and takes you smoothly and efficiently into the future. For marketing to work, you can't choose a piece here and a piece there and expect results. It is the overall program that makes the difference.

Marketing today is not an option. Companies that practice good marketing grow, thrive, and prosper. They commit the necessary resources because they see marketing as their investment in the future. So, on your mark, get set, go!

Chapter
FIVE

———— ✧ ————

Telling Your Story

The Secrets of
Self-Promotion

*Graham's Law: If you don't tell your story,
why should you expect anyone to know what
you sell?*

HOW TO BE OMNIPRESENT

Many photocopier manufacturers have a strange notion—they seem to think that business people are just standing around waiting to get rid of their existing copy machines. Like the coming of the four seasons, the one thing you can be sure of throughout the year is a steady stream of cold calls and unsolicited visits from copier salespeople.

In most cases, switching copy machines is about the last thing on your mind. And when you actually are ready to buy a new copier, you'll probably go to the Yellow Pages and start calling vendors for competitive quotes. This means that all those cold calls were wasted, with the rare exception of any that happened to coincide with your decision to buy a new machine.

This raises an interesting dilemma. On the one hand, no company can afford to have sales reps call on you every month. On the other hand, even if you could, no customer would want to hear from your salespeople so frequently. The challenge, then, is to solve the riddle of "simultaneously being there without being there." The best solution we know of is to launch and maintain a vigorous, continuous self-promotional campaign.

What is self-promotion? It includes all those activities that a company undertakes to tell its own story. The possibilities for self-promotion could fill an entire book. Here we'll only discuss the basic tools that any company can use to inform the world about its products, services, and special abilities. These include newsletters, direct mail, trade shows, marketing seminars, special events, informational and capabilities brochures, and other collateral materials.

While every company must determine which self-promotional tools will best meet its needs, in the end it's the mix of tools that makes the difference. If the mix is right, a self-promotion campaign will get and keep your company exactly where you want it—in front of your customers at all times. Then, when your customer is ready to buy, you'll be the vendor of choice.

In other words, the mix of self-promotional tools extends your reach through time and space. A good campaign will place a "salesperson" in the customer's mind 52 weeks a year. Properly designed and executed, your self-promotional tools won't be seen as intrusive by customers and prospects. To the contrary, customers will actually *look forward* to receiving your materials and meeting you at trade shows.

The next sections describe each of the basic self-promotional tools that any company can readily put into action and explores how they can be used to achieve your customer cultivation goals.

NEWSLETTERS

Of all the self-promotion tools, few are as potentially effective—and often misused—as newsletters. Many companies view a newsletter as nothing more than an advertising supplement. And they wonder why customers and prospects don't do cartwheels when the newsletter arrives. These are the same people who say, "Newsletters don't work."

In reality, a newsletter is a special communication vehicle that allows you to talk to your customers on a consistent basis in ways that you can't achieve through advertising, brochures, direct mail, cold calls, or office visits. Here's why. Every company acquires experience, skills, and specialized knowledge from helping customers solve problems. A good newsletter will take that knowledge and translate it into helpful information that any existing customer or prospect can put to good use.

Some people object to the concept of communicating valuable information to the world, saying, "Sure. And give away all our trade secrets? That's dumb." In fact, what you're really doing with a well-designed newsletter is revealing your competence—which is what customers are looking for in a supplier. That's smart, since you'll be perceived as both helpful and knowledgeable. A good newsletter can become a key customer cultivation tool because it:

- *Establishes your expertise.* A newsletter lets your customers get inside your head and appreciate the depth and extent of your knowledge. The more customers and prospects see your company as a source of expertise, the greater the chance you will become the vendor of choice. Also, if you take the time and effort to produce a high-quality product, it means you're a high-quality company.

- *Maintains ongoing communications.* The monthly or quarterly newsletter places you squarely in the customer's mind at regular, scheduled intervals. This improves the chances that when the customer is ready to buy, he'll turn to you.

- *Provides a means for informing customers, over a period of time, about all your products and capabilities.* Newsletters can be just the cure for the "Hey, I didn't know you do that" blues. That's because they enable you to describe your full range of products and services in a non-self-serving context. Remember, the goal of the newsletter is to pass along information, not to sell a product.

- *Gives you a competitive edge over companies that merely see themselves as a pipeline for passing along goods and services to customers.* A newsletter allows you to shine like a bright star in a dark sky. It enables you to create your market position, rather than have one handed to you by your competitors. Also, if you take the time and effort to produce a high-quality product, it tells the world that you're a high-quality company.

How to Start and Maintain an Effective Newsletter

While every company should develop its own unique newsletter look, feel, and editorial policy, certain success factors apply to any newsletter, regardless of the nature of the company's business. The following newsletter "universals" fall into four separate, yet interrelated categories: Support, Editorial, Design/Production, and Distribution.

Support

Before you launch a newsletter, make sure you have the necessary resources (people, money, equipment) to do the job. The only thing worse than a shoddy newsletter is a vanishing newsletter. If you start and then kill a newsletter, you're telegraphing a bad message to your customers or clients. You're really saying that you don't have the ability to follow through with important projects. So you're better off not doing a newsletter than only assembling the resources to do a trial run. Be prepared to make a long-term commitment.

One step that companies often overlook is the need for professional graphic design and layout, either from an in-house graphics person or an outside consultant (see below). Another aspect of support concerns editorial resources. While you don't need a full-time editorial staff to write your newsletter, you also can't dump the writing responsibilities on a department secretary. Find someone who has the inside knowledge of your company, the writing skills, and the necessary time to make the newsletter happen. If the newsletter is tremendously successful, you might want to hire a full-time writer later.

Also, have an editorial review board in place. If the review process is like a floating crap game, with the responsibility passing from manager to manager each month or quarter, then you're only asking for turf and ego battles. Establish a board of knowledgeable people who can quickly scan the newsletter copy with an eye for technical accuracy and company policy.

Finally, if you're going to produce the newsletter yourself, be prepared to invest in sufficient training for people who will use the typesetting or desktop publishing equipment. Otherwise, you'll wind up farming out the production at the last minute at premium rates.

In short, don't proceed with a newsletter unless you're serious about it. The magnetic effects sometimes don't kick in until you have published five or six issues. If this is too long for your return on investment criteria, then newsletters (and most other customer cultivation tools) will be too poky for your taste.

Editorial

As we mentioned earlier, the biggest mistake people make is treating their newsletters as ad rags. If you take this attitude, you're just wasting trees to print circulars that at best will grace the floors of your customer's bathroom stalls. To create a newsletter that people actually *want* to read, use the following guidelines:

1. *Provide information of immediate use to the reader.* No one gives a hoot about who was promoted to president or who won the Employee of the Year award. Nor do they care that you've just sold your one billionth paper clip. What they do want to hear is:

   - How you solved problems for other customers
   - New ways to use your products or services
   - Tips for using your products or service to increase their efficiency, productivity, profitability, and competitive position
   - Expert advice that pertains to their industry

   You can convey this kind of information through two basic techniques. One is the case study approach, in which you describe a typical problem that a customer faced and how they solved it using your product or services. Tell the story through the customer's eyes, not your own. In fact, resist all temptation to blow your own horn; let the story do that for you in a subtle way. If you do use a case study approach, mention the customer's name (assuming you have permission—most customers will love it!). This has a tremendous effect on the article's credibility.

The second technique is to have an outside expert write a feature article or supply information for a feature article. For example, let's say that your company manufactures an analytical device used in medical labs. Publish a piece describing a particularly pesky problem that lab technicians must deal with when performing the analysis, regardless of what brand equipment they're using. Of course, the implication is that since your company provides solutions, it is the company to buy from. And by publishing the article under an outsider's name, you have the necessary distance to establish credibility.

2. *Provide a good mix of information.* Few people have the time or inclination to read a single six- or eight-page article. Ideally, your newsletter should be four pages, with a feature article occupying about a page and a half at most. Devote the rest to "short takes" and "tidbits" of information, of the "helpful hints from Heloise" variety. Again, keep the information relevant. You might, for example, provide:

- Information about new management techniques
- Industry and business trends
- Explanations about the technology behind a breakthrough product
- A calendar of upcoming seminars, conferences, trade shows, and so on
- Book reviews
- Specialty software program reviews

3. *Encourage reader participation.* By all means, publish letters from readers. A "Question & Answer Forum" is even better. Invite people to send in problems, so you can publish solutions. There is no better way to guarantee that your newsletter will be read.

4. *Maintain your neutrality.* Never accept advertising or classifieds from readers, even if they represent your best accounts. The slightest appearance that you have an axe to grind or brand to push will immediately destroy your hard-earned credibility.

   A related issue is the use of response cards (business reply cards perforated into the newsletter). If you're using the newsletter to find new prospects, keep your response card simple. Use it to ask people whether they want to stay on the mailing list. Do a separate mailing to the prospects to see if they want additional product or service literature. But whatever you do, keep the newsletter squeaky "clean."

5. *Never let the newsletter become the President's pet project— it might quickly degenerate into a dog in search of a pound.* To succeed, the newsletter must be customer oriented. That means rigorously focusing on topics that the customer wants to read about. If a founder, owner, or senior manager co-ops the newsletter, you can be sure that customers will soon be reading company hype. But not for long.

Design/Production

The old saying, "You only get one chance to make a first impression," certainly holds true for newsletters. That's why it's critical to bring in a professional designer early in the game. Here are some design and production tips that can get you on the right track:

1. *Find your "graphic balance."* No one wants to read a newsletter that looks like it was designed by a graduate of the Rambo School of Desktop Publishing. On the other hand, if the newsletter is so slick that it oozes off the reader's desk, people are likely to regard it as a sales brochure masquerading as a neutral publication. The key, then, is to strike a balance that achieves the right look and feel for your business.

   If you're a technology company, the newsletter should be inviting and readable, yet distinctly high tech. If you're in the matchmaking business, something "warm and fuzzy" with personal flair will be in order. Whatever you do, tailor the design to your audience. Forget about what's important to you—take a little time and be sure your publication is aimed at your customers.

2. *Use lots of boxes, rules, and other visual elements to break up the text.* The highest complement you can receive is a call from someone who says, "Hey, I clipped the box on page four describing four executive stress reducers and sent it to all our managers" or "I cut out the June issue's Reader's Corner box and sent it to our engineering staff—it really helped them get a better understanding of the customer's point of view." This type of "thank you" will yield a long–term reward.

3. *Have a prominent Table of Contents or Issue Highlights Box on page one.* A Table of Contents or listing of newsletter highlights is a great way to get people to read your publication. A contents listing should not be a design or editorial afterthought—it may be the single most important element in getting your newsletter read.

4. *Fine-tune your production process.* Desktop publishing has made it economically practical to produce your newsletters in-house. But despite the ads of computer

makers, desktop publishing is not something that can be learned in 10 minutes. Or 10 hours. If you want to hit your publication schedule (which is crucial—see next section)—you can't afford to have someone spend eight hours trying to load soft fonts when, in fact, they don't have any soft fonts.

If your company has a production department or a person skilled in desktop publishing, go full speed ahead with your in-house resources. If not, bring in a consultant to teach your staff how to produce the newsletter. Alternately, farm out the newsletter to a production company until you're confident that you can meet your publication deadlines.

5. *Keep a regular schedule.* Once your customers get used to receiving your newsletter every month or quarter, you can't turn back. When the publication date comes and goes, and your newsletter is sitting in your word processor, your phone will start ringing with nasty complaints. It's straightforward Pavlovian conditioning.

Again, this means that you have to live up to your commitment—your customers have a long memory for marketing fiascos. That's why it's so important to make sure you have the resources to publish the newsletter on a regular basis. It's also a good incentive for starting off with a realistic publication schedule. If you've never published a newsletter, a monthly schedule might be a bit ambitious. Go for a quarterly schedule instead. While you can always increase the frequency to once a month, you can't go backwards without telegraphing anxieties.

Distribution

The best newsletter in the world won't yield any benefits for your company unless it reaches the right people. The following techniques will help ensure that your publication achieves your goals.

1. *Send it to everyone who comes in contact with your company.* Remember, the newsletter is first and foremost a customer cultivation tool. Anyone who reads your publication and finds something of interest may become a future customer. Therefore, it's critical to have systems in place for immediately putting prospects on your newsletter distribution list. Your receptionist, sales force, marketing staff, and customer service reps should always be on the lookout for new "subscribers." Even though one or two issues may not sell potential customers on your products or service, the repeated exposure will help make you the vendor of choice when prospects are ready to buy.

2. *Target your mailing list.* Your primary list will consist of your own customers and people who have made literature requests. You might also want to purchase lists from a broker or compile your own from directories. If you do either, be sure that each label contains an individual's name. Mail earmarked for "President," "Director of Marketing," or "Owner" invariably finds its way into the trash can.

3. *Never put the newsletter in an envelope.* By making the newsletter a self-mailer, you not only save postage, but you also convey the message that the publication should be read immediately. By not using an envelope, you also make it easier for people to eyeball your newsletter as it winds it way from the mailroom to the recipient's desk.

These guidelines can help you maximize your chances of producing a newsletter that attracts new customers and helps you keep your old ones. As with any magnet marketing tool, though, practice makes perfect—the longer you can consistently publish your newsletter, the better the chances that you'll use it to cultivate customers.

One last word of caution. If you want your newsletter to be read (and that's the purpose of publishing it in the first place), then base it on this premise: It isn't what you want to say in your newsletter that counts, it's what your reader wants to see that's important. If you follow this advice, your newsletter will get rave reviews from the readers. And you'll get a lot more business.

DIRECT MAIL

Most direct mail is oriented towards selling products or services. Which is why junk mail is just that—junk. In fact, direct mail can be an excellent customer cultivation tool if you focus on what the customer wants to hear. Far too many direct mail pieces talk about the company—how long it's been in business, why its products or services are the best, and so on.

Of course, there's always a legitimate need for mail solicitations and announcements for new products and special sales. But you can broaden your concept of direct mail to include reprints of news clips about your company, published articles that you or staff members have written, and other pieces that validate your credibility through third parties.

Several factors contribute to the effectiveness of any direct mail campaign aimed at cultivating customers:

1. *Repetition.* Mailing an occasional reprint of an article about your company won't make a lasting impact. That's why it's critical to structure a mailing program that ensures a continuous flow of self-promotional materials to customers and prospects. Remember that every day people are caught in an informational deluge. According to a study by Bell Labs, a single issue of *The*

New York Times contains more information than a 16th century adult had to contend with in his entire lifetime! So, to keep from getting lost in that flood, you've got to repeat your message as frequently as possible. Moreover, by mailing a steady stream of self-promotional materials, you greatly increase your chances that you'll be the vendor of choice when the urge to buy visits your customer.

2. *A personalized approach.* The letter you include with your mailing must be personalized. "Dear Friend" just doesn't cut it. Nor does "Dear Executive." Or any other nonspecific salutation. As with newsletter mailing lists, only labels with full names should be used in your direct mail campaign.

3. *Imagination.* Most direct mail gets tossed moments after it's opened. Try sending something to key accounts that people might actually find useful or amusing. Graham Communications sends a number of intriguing gizmos every year to potential clients. One year it sent major accounts and prospects a lucite "roulette wheel" with an arrow mounted on the front. Printed on the top of the wheel is the headline: "Nine ways for a business to get ready for the road ahead." When you spin the arrow, it will stop at one of the following stations: Take charge of your destiny; Put on blinders; Tighten your belt; Worry; Complain loudly; Take your chances; Wring your hands; Hope for the best; and Sit and wait. Executives not only love the toy, but it conveys the attitudes that most business people bring to the marketplace—and reminds them of the role that PR and marketing should take in charting the course of their companies.

Another year Graham Communications sent complementary "auto–dialers" to all new prospects. These devices, when held up to the telephone, automatically emit the tones corresponding to a single telephone number. Just hold the device to the phone, press the button, and Voila! The phone number is dialed. Guess whose number is preprogrammed into the device?

Why is this such a "great" idea? It captures the recipient's imagination—Who can resist trying it out?

TRADE SHOWS

When used as a customer cultivation technique, trade shows can become an effective means for gaining specific information about potential customers. Here are some tips to make trade shows work for you:

1. *Cultivate, don't collar.* Ever notice that at trade shows, attendees often walk down the aisles without turning their heads? They try to see what's happening out of the corner of their eye. What's behind this curious posturing? Simple. Many people feel that if they make eye contact with someone staffing a booth, they'll get snagged for a sale.

   It doesn't have to be that way. While you'd be a fool to turn away someone who's ready to buy, never forget that the most important function of a trade show is to find more customers who can be cultivated for future business. You're more likely to achieve your customer cultivation goals by putting people at ease and making them feel that you're there to inform and educate them. Of course, while you're conveying information about how you can help them solve their problems, you're subtly planting the seeds for future sales.

2. *Have Fun.* Too many trade show booths are all business and no play. Since you're trying to leave people with a

positive feeling about you and your company and the way you do business, make their encounter with your booth an entertaining one. Raffles are a time-honored way to get people involved with your display. They also provide an excellent way for you to qualify prospects before they drop their business cards into the bowl.

Of course, sales can be made at trade shows, but viewing these occasions as opportunities for customer cultivation and lead development is even more important. If you play it right at your next trade show, people may even *want* to come and visit your booth!

MARKETING SEMINARS AND SPECIAL EVENTS

Many firms, especially those in professional services, sponsor customer education seminars. Such seminars are standard cultivation tools for accounting and financial planning firms. The purpose of the sessions is twofold. First, they create yet another point of contact for your salespeople. Second, they shape the customer's perception, because they reinforce your company's expertise and give prospects a chance to see what it's like to work with your staff.

The following rules will help you get the most self-promotional mileage from your seminars.

1. *Educate first; sell second.* As with all the above-mentioned self-promotional tools, the goal is to provide useful information, not shove products or services down prospects' throats. The more useful the information, the greater the chances the prospects will become customers when they're ready to buy or have a problem to solve.

2. *Never charge an admission fee.* Once you start charging at the door, you've crossed the boundary between pro-

moting your existing business and running a seminar business. If you can't afford to sponsor the event, then don't try to compensate by charging a fee. Wait until you can afford to invest your money in something that will have a long-term payback.

3. *Keep it short.* A freebie seminar should not last more than two hours, from beginning to end. Beyond that, most busy people have to make special arrangements, which means your attendance will plummet.

4. *Use a good mix of in-house and outside resources.* Outside speakers with recognized expertise in your area can reinforce the fact that your educational intent is sincere. Also, if your firm is unknown or new, they can enhance your stature. In general, though, your own people should have the strongest presence at the show—your payoff will be significantly greater because you can communicate exactly what you want. Your own people can also build confidence among prospects, that they'll be in good hands when dealing with your company.

5. *Pick the seminar topics wisely.* It's very important to offer people information about topics near and dear to their hearts. Don't ever worry about giving away the store at a seminar—if you could exhaust your knowledge base in two hours, then you don't have much to sell anyway! And don't limit your thinking. Why should a seminar focus just on your business? Perhaps you're a distributor, in which case why not invite an articulate CPA to discuss financial issues important to your dealers? Or, ask a marketing specialist to discuss ways for dealers to improve their public relations and advertising. Once again, helpful information is what counts.

6. *Pick your attendees wisely.* When it's time to invite people to the seminar, roll out your list of prospects and ex-

isting customers. Never send an impersonal flyer or brochure. Send a formal letter or invitation that looks like the recipient was hand picked for invitation to this special occasion.

What we've described in this section would technically be called "marketing seminars." They're designed to bring both customers and prospects into a closer relationship with your company. Never forget that your most compelling sales tool at these seminars is education. Your audience will be more than satisfied if you have given them worthwhile help and valuable information.

SPECIAL EVENTS

Every company has opportunities for special events, such as open houses, anniversaries, new quarters, and so on. An open house can be particularly effective, because many customers never see their vendors and therefore only have their own mental image. By bringing customers to the source of the action, they will feel that they are dealing with real people, real equipment, and so on. This builds confidence that your company has the capabilities to make things happen.

BROCHURES

Each year, companies spend millions and millions of dollars designing, printing, and distributing brochures that are never read by anyone other than the people who wrote them. Almost without exception, nearly all the brochures proposed for businesses in any given day should never be produced, because the vast majority are irrelevant to the cultivation of customers.

Whatever the problem, most companies seem to think that the solution is a brochure. It isn't. To illustrate the point, consider the brochure of a midwestern-based engineering firm whose revenues were declining because of a slowdown in commercial real estate development. The firm's piece, designed to stanch the flow of red ink, just screamed "dollars"—six-color photographs, expensive photography, excellent printing. All told, the brochure must have cost a good $100,000.

Despite it's elegance, the brochure had some major flaws, starting with the cover, which featured a photo of a golf ball in motion. The photography was dramatic and attention-getting to say the least. But the message was confusing. "Does this company sell golf balls?" That would be a logical conclusion, and one that was not corrected by the brochure interior, which looked like a product catalog. Sadly, everything you never wanted to know about that company was there, along with clever, gimmicky photos that attracted your attention, but not your interest in the engineering firm.

All this is typical of far too many brochures. Fortunately, there are a number of easy ways to make sure your brochures don't fall into the common traps. When planning your next brochure or evaluating one that already exists, consider the following:

1. *Brochures do not make sales.* Far too often, a brochure is unconsciously viewed as a crutch or even "a substitute" for marketing. Brochures help paint a picture in the customer's mind and communicate a message that may eventually lead to a sale.

2. *Even though a brochure can't make a sale, it can make a good first impression.* In the split second that it takes to hand someone a brochure or to pull one out of an envelope, the impression is made. Although your brochure may never be read, it has done its job of presenting your company properly.

3. *When your brochure speaks, make sure it talks the customer's language.* Most brochures, like so many other business

publications, start at the wrong place because they're written from the company's viewpoint. That's why these publications are often called "capabilities brochures." No matter what, the company is going to get its story told just the way it wants to tell it. "What's wrong with that?" you might ask. Well, just about everything. Remember this: When you talk about yourself, no one listens. In fact, nobody cares. The same is true for the company that insists on filling its corporate brochure with its own message.

If you want to impress your customers with your story, then forget about what you want to say, about the message you so eagerly want to get across. All that's irrelevant. Before you do anything else, ask yourself this question: What message does a customer want to hear?

In order to get the proper perspective, it will be helpful to actually talk to some customers. Should you choose this unconventional route, you will find out exactly what's important to the people who support you. You'll then be in a position to answer the questions that customers want to hear: What problems can you solve for them? How can you increase their productivity? Decrease their costs? Reduce their overhead? Save them time? Avoid unnecessary delays? And so on. Your solutions will catch your customers' attention. They are the "stuff" out of which great brochures are made (because they get read).

4. *Let your customers tell your story.* A brochure built around customer comments and interviews packs a lot of power. Instead of publishing an endless array of boring full-color photos of company executives, focus on your satisfied customers. Let them tell your story— you'll get maximum credibility.

One common objection to featuring customers in brochures, ads, and newsletters is based on a fear of giving away "secret" information. "We don't want our competition to know about our customers," critics contend. "They'll go after them." On the surface, this sounds very businesslike and protective. In reality, it's nonsense. If your competitors don't already know who you're doing business with, then they aren't really competing.

Finally, customers are pleased to be singled out for inclusion in your brochure. It lets them know you value your relationship with them, not just their business. What will customers who are not included in your brochure say? Some customers may actually give you more business hoping you'll feature them in your next revision!

If you follow these guidelines, you'll maximize the chances that your brochure will be readable and read. Most important, you will probably stimulate interest and allow the reader to get acquainted with how you do business. Even though a brochure will not make a sale, it can pave the way to future sales, answer questions, and create a more beneficial selling environment.

Self-promotion, in the form of the tools discussed in this chapter, is a powerful marketing weapon. But only if used correctly. With hundreds of messages bombarding your customers and prospects every day, you need an aggressive program to have an impact on your audience. By coordinating a variety of self-promotional activities, you'll begin to get the kind of results you need to gain a competitive advantage. In Chapter 6, you'll learn how to complement your self-promotional activities with a strong media relations campaign.

———— ✧ ————

Meeting the Press

How to Structure an Effective Media Relations Campaign

Graham's Law: If you think the media is the enemy, you don't know a friend when you see one.

TAKING ADVANTAGE OF MEDIA OPPORTUNITIES

Most people have never heard of Thomas Jefferson Beale. Warren Holland hadn't either, until he read an article describing how Beale planted a chest full of money in the Blue Ridge Mountains during the late 1800s, then left a code for would-be treasure hunters. Apparently, he found it great fun.

Holland decided that he too could have great fun by instigating a national treasure hunt. So he gave up his construction business and spent six months studying the art of creating ciphers—codes made up of letters and numbers. Then, he created a jigsaw puzzle called Decipher.

The back of each piece contained numbers and letters. When the whole puzzle was assembled, it spelled out a cipher message. To help people crack the code, Holland provided a "clue," embedded in a novel by one of twenty-one authors mentioned in the instructions. Holland offered $100,000 reward that would be shared by all those who cracked the cipher by a certain date. Thirty-six people shared in the $100,000 reward, but not before Holland sold more than 200,000 copies of the game.

What's most remarkable about this story is that Holland didn't spend a dime on paid advertising. He brilliantly captured the attention of the national media, which provided the equivalent of a high-priced ad campaign. That, of course, paid off handsomely on the bottom line.

Holland's case is extreme, in that his entire marketing campaign consisted of media coverage. Most companies will not have such a luxury, and media relations will serve as but one element of its customer cultivation tool kit. Nevertheless, good media coverage is a highly cost-effective method of attracting and keeping customers and should be pursued energetically.

Positive press coverage is invaluable because it carries the writer's and publisher's seals of approval. Third party endorsement generates the kind of credibility that you can't create with your own literature. Be aware, though, that media relations takes time and there's no instant payoff. You can't just fire off a press release and wait for *The Wall Street Journal, Business Week,* and *Forbes* to write feature stories about your company. A continuing media relations effort will, however, reap unprecedented results in establishing your company's leadership in the marketplace.

In this chapter, we'll explore numerous opportunities for developing positive press coverage that can promote your company as the vendor of choice. Note that if you're looking for techniques for exploiting the press or using it as a free advertising vehicle, you'll be disappointed. And you should be— the press isn't your private bulletin board. If you don't have something newsworthy or valid, don't expect the media to say it for you. Rather, this chapter describes the general process of finding newsworthy topics within the four walls of your company. It also lays out two approaches to developing media relations: getting reporters to take your lead and publishing "bylined articles."

STEPPING INTO THE LIMELIGHT

Every day you read news stories that quote business people from a variety of industries. This does not happen by accident—corporate PR departments and PR agents are constantly feeding reporters and editors the kind of information they need to make their jobs easier. Moreover, every company has expertise and harbors some story that can be told in a fascinating way. "So you just make widgets?" In the right hands, the widget story could become the thriller of the year. Just look at Tracy Kidder's *House,* a full-length book about the design and building of a single family home in rural Massachusetts. Ho hum? Bestseller! Or consider Louis Malle's *My Dinner With Andre,* a feature length, critically acclaimed film that consists of two guys talking over a meal.

The point is, if you believe that your company isn't doing anything of interest to the rest of the world, then you're missing a wealth of media opportunities right under your nose.

Before presenting techniques for exploiting media opportunities, however, we will review some of the reasons that business people actually avoid the media, and present counterarguments. You might agree that positive press is extremely valuable, but if you're gun shy about reporters, then your company will never make its way into print.

Overcoming Media Phobia

Making news is not the primary goal of most business people. In fact, there's a strong tendency for those in business to try to avoid the news spotlight:

"You're always quoted out of context."
"I never said that."
"All they want is to sell papers."
"You can't trust anyone from the press."

Such refrains are often heard when talking with business people about the news media. Actually, each one of these remarks is essentially correct! Let's analyze them one at a time.

- *You're always quoted out of context.* Unfortunately, this does happen. But there's often a good explanation: either no one bothered to place the remarks in the proper context or no one provided the necessary background information so the reporter could put the views expressed in perspective. This problem can be eliminated if you plan ahead and *shape* the media to your needs.

- *I never said that.* Most people are surprised when they see their words in print. As we speak, we know what we

85

mean; unfortunately, others may not. So what we said and what we think we said are often at odds.

- *All they want to do is sell papers.* Frankly, that's not such a bad goal. How many newspapers you sell is an important measure of success. And it's much better being quoted in a successful paper than an unsuccessful one. Yet, behind this particular comment is the notion that every reporter is out to get you. Not true. Good reporters should ask probing questions. Good reporters should dig into the implications of your words. That's what makes us squirm.

- *You can't trust anyone from the press.* If anything, there's a basic distrust of the press on the part of most business people. And that's not surprising—it's the dark and seamy stories of corporate corruption and the escapades of boardroom blockheads that make for headlines. No one wants to read about companies that play fair and square, maintain high standards of ethics, and actually care about their customers. But you can't let that issue scare you away. Unless you're harboring some terrible skeletons in your corporate closet, chances are that you'll enjoy great benefit from press exposure.

  Also, if you're in business, you like to feel that you're in control. Therefore, being "at the mercy" of someone such as a reporter makes you feel uneasy. That's why it's quite common for a person in business to ask to review a reporter's story before it's printed.

  In reality, "trust" is not the issue at all. Business people have a tendency to want to express their own version of reality. Reporters have learned that "facts" are not always factual and one way or another figures get altered. Only those details considered "appropriate" are provided to the press, while anything considered possibly "embarrassing" is held back. In the final analysis, the press has a right to be suspicious of the business community!

As you can see, the common excuses for staying away from the press don't hold up. So, assuming you're ready to meet the press, read on for a discussion of how to find aspects of your company that will attract newspaper and magazine editors.

WORKING WITH THE MEDIA

As we've stressed, published news stories carry with them instant credibility. Being in the news can establish a sense of leadership that is difficult to create in any other way. In effect, the press is the business community's best friend.

Good press relations opens the extraordinary possibility for communicating your message to customers, prospects, associates, stockholders, and employees in a highly effective and impressive way. To fail to use the press to tell a newsworthy story is to miss one of the best opportunities available to business today.

Being successful with the press requires an understanding of how to work effectively with editors by recognizing their needs. This comes down to successfully cultivating editors, just as you cultivate customers. The process does not happen overnight, so if your ship is taking on water, don't look to the media as a life preserver. Editors and reporters are smart enough to spot the rats departing for dry ground and have no interest in sponsoring a rescue mission.

Cultivating the media involves three types of activities:

1. Discovering what editors and reporters are working on, what they will be working on in the future, and how you can fit into their plans.

2. Developing new and interesting angles about your company, the kind that will excite editors and reporters.

3. Conveying key information to the media in a format that enables editors and reporters to easily write up your story.

Methods for making each activity a success are described below.

Getting Inside the Media

There's no great secret to synchronizing your press materials with the interests of reporters and editors. All you have to do is pick up the phone or write a letter. Specifically:

1. *Check the editorial calendars.* Most business publications will gladly give you their editorial calendars. These are primarily prepared for advertisers who want to decide the issues in which they should purchase space. A quick review of an editorial calendar should give you ideas about events going on in your own company that might be of interest to the publication, such as the acquisition of a breakthrough technology, a new community outreach, a new employee preventive health program, and so on.

2. *Avail your expertise.* Always think in terms of "inside" information that you can volunteer to the press when an event breaks or a particular subject suddenly becomes popular. The more your information helps to further the public's understanding or appreciation of the issues, the greater the chance the press will use it. At the same time, the fact that your company is in the news gives it an immeasurable credibility boost.

   Consider how newsletter publisher Richard Golob deftly managed information to gain worldwide press coverage in the wake of the *Exxon Valdez* oil spill. An internationally known expert on oil spills, and the publisher of *Golob's Oil Pollution Bulletin*, he immediately turned to his database when news of the spill first trickled in over the wire services. Within hours, he had sent dozens of "FAX alerts" to the major electronic and print media sources. The alert provided invaluable information that placed the Valdez oil spill in historical context, including the details of previous spill incidents (the largest spills in the United States, the largest spills worldwide, the most expensive spills to clean up, and so on). As the event unfolded, Golob continued to issue tidbits from his database, which further solidified his credentials as the key authority on the topic.

Golob's efforts quickly paid handsome dividends, which included appearances on CBS, NBC, and ABC prime time news, mentions in *The New York Times*, *The Wall Street Journal*, *Time*, and *U.S. News & World Report*, and an interview in a special NOVA film on oil spills. All the exposure helped Golob rapidly expand his subscriber base and further entrench him as one of the world's leading experts on oil spill issues.

If you're successful at cultivating the press, as Richard Golob was, you'll be elevated to the status of "known authority." This means that the media will come to *you* for help with stories when the need arises.

For example, once a year the IRS becomes a news item. At that time, reporters, editors, and producers from Daytona Beach to Walla Walla want to localize the income tax story, so they start looking for CPAs in their cities and towns to talk about hot tax issues. If you're in the accounting business, you want your firm to be the first they contact for a comment on the latest inside advice.

By cultivating the press with news releases that demonstrate your expertise (such as a list of little-known tax preparation tips), you can become a favored source for the local print or electronic media. This will, of course, provide the kind of credibility that will bring new customers to your door.

Finding Hidden News Stories

A key factor in successful media relations is having a good sense for what is news. Just because something is important to you may not mean that it's newsworthy. The hiring of a new vice president of marketing may be earthshaking to your marketing division, but it probably won't excite anyone else in the world (other than the new vice president's mother).

1. *Be current.* One way or another, you must play off current events either by confirming or denying topics in the news. Ask yourself what is happening within your company's walls that connects you to the outside world. Editors and reporters are always open to information that's going to provide insight for their readers or challenge the *status quo.*

   For example, if the condo market is down and your real estate firm is selling condos left and right, you're bucking a trend. You're also making big news. That's exactly what Granite Bank of Quincy, Massachusetts did when it foreclosed on a condominium development in a less-than-desireable section of a nearby city. The bank lowered the price, offered a good interest rate, and required no down payment. In a press release, the president of the bank described his institution's need to dispose of the property and how the bank was willing to help people acquire their own condos.

   The release was effective, judging by the daily newspapers that picked up the story. Even though the stories described the undesirability of the area, people who would not have had any other opportunities to own their own home lined up to buy the bargain-rate units. Within a week, the bank had sold half the properties.

2. *Look under your nose.* All companies harbor potentially good news stories. To find them, you need to conduct an "internal news audit." That entails looking around at your daily operation and asking the following kinds of questions:

   - *Is it unusual?* The old "man bites dog" motif still attracts news, particularly in the daily press. When a commercial bank was fined $50,000 by the federal government for improper cash transaction procedures, the Chairman of the Board asked for advice on how to handle the press. Our advice was to tell the truth, something that no one expects today. When the reporters arrived, the Chairman uttered a sentence that made headlines. "We were wrong," he stated. Unusual to be sure, but the words created such credibility with both the press and depositors that the story actually increased the stature of the bank.

   - *Can you dramatize it?* A major developer threatened the existence of a commuter boat service in Boston harbor by closing down the wharf where the boats docked. Through a series of news stories, it soon became clear that a well-heeled Goliath was trying to slay little David. By painting a picture of the developer as greedy, heartless, and uncaring, the commuter boat operator won back his docking rights.

   - *Can you create an event?* If you're the Rotary Club of Columbus and you want to attract new members, do something that will be sure to gain the media's attention. Sponsor a pancake breakfast, but with the following twist: get the city to close off a block so you can use it to serve the world's longest pancake. Or waffle. Or piece of French toast.

- *Are you sitting on an information gold mine?* Without realizing it, you might have information of great interest to the outside world. You might also be in a good position to easily acquire information that will ignite a reporter's interest. Graham Communications, for example, once conducted a survey about business meetings, just out of curiosity. We were particularly interested in what executives dislike about them. The unanimous winner in the "Major Irritant Department" was a lack of an agenda. Another big rub was people arriving unprepared. Once we compiled our results, we issued a press release announcing the findings. Reports on the results were published in the business press across the country.

- *Are you approaching a milestone?* Every company reaches a number of milestones—anniversaries, public offerings, and so on—which can be made media worthy. While no one cares if your company just turned ten years old, the business world will be itching to learn how, for the past decade, your company has managed to prosper despite a general slump in your industry. Or how your company has not only survived, but grown in the face of competition from countries in the Pacific Rim. Find the hook and cast your line, using your milestone as a wrapper for your news.

As you can see, it's not really hard to find interesting things about your company. The trick is to step outside your own head and try to view your company as an outsider. When you do that, you'll find that many things you normally take for granted are really very exciting. It's just a matter of gaining the right perspective.

Getting Information into the Right Hands

Even though you are concerned primarily with your own situation, you should have an understanding of the pressures on editors and reporters. Whether it's a daily, weekly, or monthly publication, it is a monumental task to create a new product each time the presses roll. Consequently, when editors or reporters receive your media kit, they may look for the first excuse to toss it out, rather than hunt for hidden nuggets.

Here are some techniques for enhancing the probability that your press material makes its way into print:

1. *Keep it short.* Two pages max. No exceptions. If you can't say it in two pages, then find someone who can.

2. *Send it to a specific name.* An envelope bearing the label "Editor" or "Producer" flashes a strong message: "Throw me out unopened." If you're sending out a local mailing, call up the various newspapers and radio/TV stations to get the correct names of editors, reporters, and producers. If you're embarking on a national campaign, use current directories, such as those offered by Standard Rate & Data Service (SRDS— Wilmette, IL) or Bacon's Publishing Company (Chicago, IL).

3. *Present valid information.* Editors and producers get thinly veiled advertising garbage all the time masquerading as news. They're also hypersensitive about being exploited by the business world and will resent being assaulted with more self-serving pap.

4. *Don't try to reshape facts.* Business people commonly make the mistake of thinking that they can reconstruct reality to suit their needs. Be aware that we are still very much operating in the post-Watergate era, so no one

trusts anything about anyone, especially politicians and business executives.

5. *Take a point of view.* Many business people come off sounding as bland as a bowl of rice cereal. Why? Because they're afraid to present a point of view. They refuse to take a stand. Lee Iacocca has definite ideas and doesn't hesitate to speak them. Whether or not people agree with him, they respect him for standing up for something—and he gets attention in the press.

6. *Use headlines that will grab readers by the lapels and rattle their teeth.* There are many schools of thought on writing effective press releases, but every expert agrees on one thing: if you don't capture the editor's or producer's attention immediately, you've lost the game.

7. *Establish a goal for your release.* A press release can be tailored to achieve two different objectives: luring the media to your office or getting your release published in its entirety. The first is much easier and entails using the news release as a teaser that will get the media to come to you.

   Richard Golob, mentioned earlier, used this technique when he metered out his information in small enough chunks that required the media to come to him for more information as the oil from the *Exxon Valdez* crept down the Alaskan coast. Had he given away the store in one release, he would have lost his hold on those reporting the news.

   The second goal, getting your press release printed in its entirety, is more difficult. It can only be achieved when the release is well-written, well-researched, and not obviously self-serving. If you can meet these criteria, some reporters and editors will appreciate receiving an "instant article," and you may find yourself quickly in print.

8. *Don't evaluate your ideas.* Editors don't like to be told what constitutes a good story. If an editor isn't interested in your story today, gracefully back off and submit another idea at a later time. Your ultimate goal is to build a good rapport that leads to a long-term relationship.

These tips will help you maximize your chances of getting into print or on the air waves. In any case, be patient. A constant flow of press releases to the right people will eventually tap a rich vein. While you're waiting to hit the motherload, never bug an editor, reporter, or producer—the pressure you apply will be inversely proportional to the likelihood of your getting into print or invited to comment on radio or television. Media people have a knee-jerk reaction when they feel that someone is trying to manipulate them. Follow up once and ask if you can supply any additional information. Then leave it at that and get on to writing your next release. Or sit down and try writing your own articles, as described in the next section.

THE BYLINED ARTICLE

How to Create Your Own Media Coverage

In addition to coverage by newspeople, you can take advantage of an often overlooked media relations tool, the "bylined article." These are written by or for you and marketed to the press with your name on them. Bylined articles have great value to a company because they position you as experts in a particular field, along with building excellent credibility.

Graham Communications is living proof of the effectiveness of the bylined article. In one year alone, 33 of the company's articles were published in more than 50 periodicals ranging from regional business magazines to *Fortune*—a total of 154 insertions.

These articles, which conveyed valuable tips about sales and marketing, have brought in a constant flow of leads and indicate to our existing clients that we have expertise in the field. It is also one of the main reasons Graham Communications has never had to make a single cold call. When one client signed up, he said, "If you can market my company half as well as you market yours, you'll do wonders for us!"

This is what we've learned about getting bylined articles into the media and compelling readers to pick up the phone:

1. *Write for the reader and don't push your product or service.* Don't turn your article into an ad by talking about yourself. Articles must stand on their own merit. If the ideas are timely, useful, and legitimate, then your firm will fare well in the marketplace.

2. *Be candid and direct.* Show some daring and go out on a limb—it's the only way your message will get across. Be willing to take a position and expose your ideas to the critical eyes of editors and readers. Sure, you'll get a little grief, but that only forces you to sharpen your argument.

3. *Be specific.* Organize your thoughts in order to give the reader helpful suggestions for taking action. That's what people want and expect—seven ways, 11 reasons, 14 questions. Break your ideas down into small parts. This gives the reader concrete, usable information.

4. *Choose publications that reach the right audience.* Getting into print is only part of the goal—you want to be in print in the *right* places. Select publications with readers who will be your potential customers or clients. Use an SRDS or Bacon directory (see above) to get the ad-

dresses of the publications to which you want to submit your articles.

5. *Bend over backwards to satisfy editors.* If you submit quality articles, editors may eventually call you and request specific articles. At that point, you have a priceless advertising channel aimed directly at your core audience.

   Many times an editor will want an article tailored to fit a specific requirement. Be willing—and enthusiastic—about taking the extra time required to produce a custom article.

6. *Keep your "pride of authorship" under control.* Your goal is to meet the needs of editors, not satisfy your ego. Sure it's great to see your name in print, but it's not going to get there unless you play ball with your editor. Since writing probably isn't your primary business, pay attention and you might actually learn something!

7. *Don't start writing if you can't learn to cope with rejection.* It's always a little rough when an editor says "no." But it's going to happen, probably more than once. If your sense of self-esteem depends on acceptance of everything you do, then submitting bylined articles is not a good idea for you. Stick to something with a safer returns on the emotional investment, like raising gerbils.

When you begin having a track record, it is important to analyze why certain articles are published more than others—and vice versa. The goal is to figure out what it takes to make an article a winner. Of course, there will be some articles that you assumed would be sure fire winners and didn't receive much attention. At the same time, you'll publish articles that you thought had a narrow audience and suddenly find they've been reprinted a dozen times. That happened with Graham Communications' "How to Keep Customers Coming Back." We thought it might be accepted by only one or two publications and we were shocked to see it in print in at least a dozen newsletters and magazines that we knew of.

Fringe Benefits

A lot of time and effort can go into writing, editing, distributing, and evaluating articles. It takes even more time to respond to those who call and write in response to your articles. But the end result will be well worth it in terms of attracting new customers and affirming bonds of loyalty with old ones.

Finally, writing bylined articles will provide a spinoff benefit for your company. Every time an article is published, you'll sense that your day-to-day work for customers and clients is even more important because it is set against a framework of recognition created by being a highly published firm—you'll actually be influencing the thinking of others. That's both a good feeling and the source of motivation to serve your public even better.

At this point, it should be clear that only a lack of imagination can separate you from media coverage that carries with it an implicit endorsement that you can't buy through paid advertising or direct mail. Before going any further in this book, try this little experiment. Pick up a business publication and clip a few articles that mention companies and/or executives. Imagine that you were the genius PR consultant responsible for grabbing the media's attention. Reflect on the steps you might have taken to get your clients into print. Now apply that same line of thinking to your own company.

When you're finished, you'll be ready to read about the last component of a magnet marketing program: paid advertising. While a mention in the media offers special credibility, paid advertising is nonetheless an important complement, because you can *control* when it appears. In the best of all worlds, media coverage will coincide with your paid advertising program.

But the prudent business person knows that you can only count on those things you can make happen with your check-book. That's why paid advertising is a key item in the magnet marketeer's tool kit.

Chapter
SEVEN

◇

Reaching the Masses with Advertising

The Art of Developing a Magnetic Ad Campaign

*Graham's Law: Anyone who says,
"Advertising doesn't work," has been running
a lousy ad campaign.*

RECONSIDERING THE AD GAME

According to common wisdom, when you have to sell something, you advertise. Like brochures, though, print ads and TV/radio spots are generally thought of as final solutions to marketing problems. True, a good ad can be very effective when used in conjunction with other customer cultivation tools. But by itself, an ad or series of ads is a shot in the dark that may or may not reach prospects when they're ready to buy. That's why advertising only really works when combined with self-promotion and media relations efforts. When brought together, the three sets of customer cultivation tools have a remarkable magnetic effect that far exceeds the sum of the individual components.

Since most companies don't understand the need to support advertising campaigns with other marketing tools, they often get burned and assume that advertising is a waste of money. Hence you hear the common refrain among allegedly knowledgeable marketing people: "Oh, we ran an ad back in '74 and didn't get one call. Advertising is a waste of time and money!" People who issue such proclamations rarely get around to evaluating where they placed their ads, why they placed the ad, what message their ad presented, what audience they wanted to reach, and, most importantly, why they ever thought that a "one-shot deal" would produce results.

Let's consider each of these evaluation points:

1. *Wrong media.* Even an effective ad can fail if it is placed in the wrong place. Here's a good example. In a depressed real estate market, why place an ad for condos in the classified section of a newspaper? In order for such an ad to be seen, the reader must (a) be in the market for a condo and (b) wade through page after page of advertising. A far better place to run a condo ad would be in the news section of a newspaper. Why? First, the ad will be seen by people who may not be actively in the

market for a condo. The ad may spark their interest. And second, your ad will stand out because it is not surrounded by similar ads.

2. *Wrong goals.* If you consider advertising to be a "quick fix," then it will never meet your expectations. For advertising to work, you must know exactly what you want to accomplish—in writing. Put down what you want your advertising campaign to achieve, then measure the results.

3. *Wrong message.* Ineffective advertising is based on "ego nonsense." This means that ads are conceived in terms of what the advertiser considers important. He's going to tell his story no matter what. His company is the biggest, the best, the oldest —and on and on. That's great stuff over cocktails, but it has no place in advertising because no one cares! If your goal is to impress yourself, then go ahead and waste time and money on such nonsense.

Ego-based ads reflect what the company wants to sell, not what the prospect might want to buy. But for any ad to be effective, it must reflect the customers' interests. Just pick up any business magazine, and you'll find plenty of examples of ego-based advertising, such as the full page ad featuring a rather exquisite color photo of the latest office chair. Underneath is the headline: *The Innovative Company in Ergonomics.* Who cares about this "innovative" company! Not one word about the customer's poor aching back and the endless hours he or she must sit in a chair. The ad agency that "sold" this one had an easy job. They knew the real "customer" —the chair manufacturer. It appears that the goal was to make sure the ad got sold—not the chairs.

Once you're over the "we're wonderful" hurdle, become an educator. Convey the fact that you can solve problems by providing your expertise and valuable information, not just products or services.

4. *Wrong expectations.* How many times have businesses run an ad once and come to the conclusion that advertising is a waste of money. An ad must run from three to seven times. On TV, frequency is even more important, because the images are so fleeting. Therefore, for advertising to work, there must be a commitment to an appropriate campaign.

As you can see, it is easy to come to the wrong conclusions about advertising. But to avoid advertising because of previous failures is to miss both an essential ingredient of the marketing mix and the benefits that a powerful cultivation tool can bring to your products or services.

CREATING EFFECTIVE ADS

The major task in developing effective advertising is to make sure your ads reflect your customer cultivation goals. When that happens, your advertising will become an essential tool for building sales, extending your market, and giving you the edge over your competitors. It can also make the work of your sales force both easier and more productive. All you have to do is use it correctly. The following guidelines can help to make certain your advertising will work for you:

1. *Always start with the customer or prospect.* Successful advertising begins inside the customer's head. To see why this is important, compare current advertisements for Infinity, Nissan's high-end luxury sedan, and Lexus, Toyota's entry into the Mercedes market.

   Nissan's ads for Infiniti feature lovely photography and copy designed to set your emotional gears in motion. In one ad, for example, Nissan asks you to project your mind five years into the future and imagine what kind of service the ideal auto dealer will provide. It even suggests that you think about the car as an "agreement to provide the highest level of service for as long as you own the automobile." Next to the copy, a stream meanders through a full-page full-color photograph. Nice, but what does that have to do with the car?

Lexus ads, in contrast, focus on the issue most important to the customer: What do you get for your money—today. They're simple and to the point; when you buy a Lexus, you get a cross between a BMW and a Mercedes, for a lot less money.

To avoid creating pretty ads that don't strike the "responsive chord" necessary to make a sale, pull out the following checklist before you develop a concept, design the layout, or write copy:

- *What's going on inside the customer's head?* Before you do anything else, make sure you understand what the readers are thinking.

- *What does the customer want?* Some want low price, while others want to brag about having the latest equipment. It may take more than one ad to address the issues. So attack one customer segment at a time.

- *What problems can you solve?* If you're advertising a retirement-type community, you may want to avoid "pretty pictures" of houses or condos and zero in on comfort and convenience, as well as security and friendliness. In other words, your retirement village makes life enjoyable and easier.

2. *Pick your media carefully.* Never base your buying decision solely on the price of the ad or the air time. There's a good reason why some publications offer bargain basement ad rates and their salespeople can give you "a great deal"—no one reads, listens, or views them. Base

your buying decision on whether or not the media reaches the right people. If you can't afford the right media, then wait until you have the necessary funds.

Also, it is often best to advertise in several places at the same time in order to maximize impact. Even if you're running your ad for a limited period of time, those who see it will think you're everywhere.

3. *Don't skimp on production.* You're competing with other businesses for the attention of the reader, viewer, or listener. If it's results you are looking for, then investing in a quality ad is well worth the cost. Don't buy into the idea that it's better to get a mediocre ad into print or onto the air waves than to do nothing. The public has a long memory, and once you're typed as a Class D operation, it's hard to change that image.

4. *Build an advertising schedule.* Just because you want to sell something doesn't mean everyone has a need to buy from you— at the moment. Think about how decisions are made. When people need a product or a service they tend to go with the company that comes to mind when the need arises. Not even the best salesperson can always be in the right place at the right time. But staying in front of prospects on a regular basis can position you when the right moment arises. Advertising can help position you as the vendor of choice—as long as you can commit to repeated exposure.

5. *Make it easy for the prospect to respond.* Whether it is an "800" number or a coupon for free literature, give the interested person an easy means for pursuing further information. One of the best methods to get a positive response is to offer a free educational brochure in every ad. The title might go something like this: "Twelve questions you should ask before investing in swamp land." Or, "Seven ways to improve productivity." Your

expertise can be of value to prospects and customers. Share it with them. This positions you as knowledgeable, helpful, and service oriented.

6. *Choose the right size for your ad.* Small ads can be effective for general consumer marketing, but in business-to-business advertising, anything smaller than a quarter page will not be seen or taken seriously. Always go for a full page ad whenever you can afford it—it *does* make a difference.

FINDING THE "MYSTERY CUSTOMER"

For advertising to be effective, you have to know who you want to reach. On the surface, this seems like a simple task. Just ask most company presidents, sales managers, or marketing directors to identify their customers and they'll quickly hand you a computer printout. "These are the people who do business with us," they'll say.

In fact, more often than not, the people who purchase from a company aren't the real customers. They are called "customers" and they are thought of by everyone as "our customers." But when you take a closer look, these aren't the company's customers at all. In fact, most businesses have a number of hidden "customers." You will only find them when you get below the surface. It is these "customers" who exert profound influence on how a business operates.

"I showed the proposed ad copy to my wife and she doesn't like it," said the president of a large manufacturing firm. Although he certainly did not realize what he was saying, he was letting it be known that a key customer of his company was none other than his wife!

Then there's the vice president of marketing of a large insurance agency who was working on a new ad concept. "Let's do something different," he said to the ad agency working with him. "I want our company's ads to be distinctive, not just carbon copies of the ads that our competitors run."

The project moved ahead with great interest and enthusiasm. The marketing manager and the president both approved the ad step by step from concept, to copy, and then to final design. The photography was given their final approval, too, and the mechanical was sent off by overnight mail to the four publications they had selected for insertions. "Victory" was the word on everyone's mind.

Then came the telephone call to the ad agency. It was the marketing director. "Could you come over right away," he said somewhat frantically. "The owners have changed their minds. They want to have more pictures of our staff. You know what I mean." There was no problem understanding what he meant. The translation was easy. The president wanted more photos of himself and his three sons, all vice presidents, to grace the pages of the ad!

Who was the customer in this situation? Not someone buying an insurance policy from the agency. Not at all. The real customer was the president. The ad was ultimately designed and produced to reflect his wishes.

These aren't isolated cases. Thumb through just about any magazine and the real customers will come jumping out at you. "We're the industry leader...," "Our Ionizing Litter Box Is State of the Art...," "Our prices are the lowest in the industry...." The list goes on and on.

In order to keep your eye and mind on the customer, rather than the person footing the bill, you have to stand back from the forest and see the trees. Here are three important guidelines for achieving clear, straight ad thinking. Ask:

1. *What qualities does a customer want in the companies with which it does business?* This must be a fundamental starting point, whether you're putting together an ad, newsletter, brochure, or seminar. Do you really under-

stand what's inside your customer's head or are you simply assuming that what's important to you will be as interesting and important to someone else. The best way to answer this question is to go straight to the horse's mouth—talk to your customers.

2. *What messages are important to your customers?* What are the customer's needs and how can you satisfy them? Take a good look at your ads (or brochures or newsletters). Are they filled with information about your company? Are they focusing on the customer or are they just trying to impress people?

3. *What sets you apart from your competitors?* If price is the only factor differentiating your company from the rest of the pack, you know who the real customer is. Focus on how your company solves problems and applies its expertise. In other words, focus your energies on why your company should be the vendor of choice.

If you follow these guidelines, you'll affect the way the marketplace perceives your company. And it is this perception, when carefully crafted, that will establish the right image in the minds of those you do business with every day. The key to continued success in advertising can only be found by constantly working to keep your eyes and mind on the *right* customers—those who buy your products and services.

AMPLIFYING THE EFFECTIVENESS OF YOUR ADS

Assuming that you've created ads that work and have targeted them at the right customer, you can still squeeze some extra juice out of your advertising dollars by reprinting your ads and mailing them, along with a personal letter, to current customers and prospects. Tell them why you are advertising and where the ad appears. They will be impressed. Also, you are sending them a signal to look for your ads in the future.

Finally, combine advertising with media stories about your company and its products and services. Add a regular newsletter. Use direct mail. The combination is different for every company because the goals and objectives vary. Yet, increased sales depend on a unified, coherent, and consistent marketing program in which advertising is a major thrust.

At this point, you have read about many tools used with the three core components of any magnet marketing program. In the following chapters, we'll look at strategies for deploying the tools in the wild and woolly world of the marketplace.

———— ✧ ————

Getting Ahead Through Customer Education

The Key Magnet Marketing Strategy

*Graham's Law: If you're not educating,
you're not selling.*

REACH OUT AND INFORM SOMEONE

In mid-December 1989, over a few days' span, fuel oil prices in Massachusetts skyrocketed from 90 cents a gallon to a dollar and a half. Most fuel oil dealers went into hiding to avoid the deluge of calls from infuriated customers. The situation for the dealers was worsened by politically savvy legislators who jumped at the opportunity to deflect spears headed their way from citizens irate over the State's fiscal woes. Even the governor called for an official probe.

In the midst of the fury, James P. Townsend, CEO of Townsend Oil Company, Inc., decided that further silence would only confirm his customers' suspicions, so he wrote a detailed letter explaining—not justifying—why costs were so high. His letter pointed out three critical factors that most press coverage had ignored.

First, the December cold spell in the Northeast lasted 30 days and was 30 percent colder than any other December on record. Second, Europe had also experienced an extraordinary early cold spell in the fall, and a lot of U.S. fuel oil was diverted there. As a result, the U.S. refineries weren't prepared for the surprise "deep freeze" at the beginning of the winter.

Finally, Townsend described how, in New England, many factories, hospitals, and other major natural gas users have an interruptible clause in their contracts with the gas companies. This clause allows the utility to force the user to switch to fuel oil if natural gas supplies are too low, which was the case in December. In short, demand far outstripped supply, and we all know what happens to prices when supply and demand are out of synch.

Townsend's letter reviewed each factor in a dispassionate way, avoiding finger-pointing, back-peddling, or any mention of blame. Within several days after mailing 5,000 letters, angry calls not only stopped but some customers even called or wrote to *thank* Townsend for taking the time to explain the situation. The cold spell passed and Townsend Oil didn't lose a single customer.

The moral of Townsend's story is that customers thrive on information. And not just during crises. Whether you're trying to keep old customers or create new ones, customer education is an essential marketing strategy. As competitive pressures continue to build in the 1990s, the factor that sets one company apart from the one next door will be the degree to which it devotes itself and its resources to marketing through the use of educational techniques.

Granted, the idea of "customer education" may produce yawns from some adrenaline-driven sales and marketing experts. After all, education doesn't sound very original or glamorous. In fact, it even has a somewhat somber ring to it. Also, sales managers want "results," so anything that takes time is viewed as irrelevant to making sales.

In spite of what some sales types may think, customer education offers the excitement of a new marketing frontier for business. It's an opportunity for you to prove that your company is as good as you say it is and that you have expertise worth sharing.

Whether it's via a newsletter, seminar, or space advertising, demonstrate that you are concerned with the customer by doing an effective job as a problem solver. Make it possible for people to learn from you. That makes an impression by creating confidence. As for results, when customers are given a predisposition to buy products or services from your company, you'll see long-term improvements to your bottom line.

In this chapter, we'll describe proven techniques for continually passing along helpful information to your customers. We'll also describe how customer education can become a strategic element in your magnet marketing program.

BEYOND THE BETTER BROCHURE

What does customer education mean? Let's start with what it *doesn't* mean: bigger and glossier brochures, or even an improved level of product knowledge. Nor are we talking about making certain customers "understand" what you sell or what you do.

Rather, customer education means taking seriously the task of making available a company's expertise and knowledge in new and creative ways. To put it simply, those businesses that want to grow and prosper in the years ahead will produce and distribute one primary product: Know-how.

More than any other single factor, knowledge invested in customers and prospects will pay the biggest dividends. This will be particularly true in the 1990s, since the strongest enterprises will be the leanest enterprises. With reductions in support staff, the responsibility for disseminating information will fall on the shoulders of those who market a company's goods or services.

MARKETING YOUR EXPERTISE

The saying, "Information is power," may be hackneyed, but it still rings true when it comes to marketing. In fact, from the standpoint of customer cultivation, marketing really boils down to getting the right information into the right hands at the right time. The right information builds credibility and naturally guides potential customers to your products and services. As a result, when prospective clients or customers call, they already know your ideas, your areas of expertise, and, most important, they perceive you as different from your competitors. At that point, your task is not to convince or persuade them to buy—they're already confident that you're the vendor of choice—but to focus your total attention on their issues, their concerns, their problems, and their opportunities.

The key benefit is that with adequate customer education, it's not necessary for you to spend time and effort on trying to "sell" a prospect on your company. That's already happened. Instead, you're free to concentrate on the needs of the prospect. This gives you a real "selling edge" and puts you far ahead of your competitors.

The goal of any customer education effort should be to support your position as an expert and an industry leader. Here are several techniques for doing just that. (You'll probably notice that some of the following ideas are similar to the self-promotion tactics described in Chapter 5. In fact, customer education should be a theme that permeates *all* of your cultivation efforts, whether they're self-promotion, media relations, or advertising.)

1. *Write purely informational articles.* An article that addresses typical customer questions and problems can have a major impact on your company's ability to attract customers. For example, Star Datacom, a telephone equipment installation firm, developed a marketing program that used the company's extensive engineering and equipment application expertise as the basis for a series of articles for business publications. The idea for the series evolved from a sales staff meeting, which revealed a common pool of questions, problems, and issues that all of the customers face.

   Star Datacom's article topics ranged from ways to avoid "telephone tag" to "getting the message with voice mail." They immediately attracted the attention of the editors of *Boardroom Reports* and other well-known publications. More important, they grabbed the attention of potential customers who felt that this company really understood the needs of nontechnical users. Over the long haul, that trust will develop into sustained sales and satisfied customers.

2. *Use advertising as an opportunity to provide useful information.* In Chapter 7 we described the importance of going beyond ego-based advertising and considering the customer perspective. Another twist on conventional advertising is using precious ad space to educate customers about important issues.

   Consider how Northwest Orient Airlines has refined this approach into a fine art. Rather than bash heads with its competitors over price or the width of its first class seats, Northwest sinks its money into ads that teach customers how to do business in Asia. For example, one insert in Fortune magazine reads, "Women doing business in Asia shouldn't reveal too much of themselves." It then explains several cultural traps that business women fall into when dealing with Asian companies. The last paragraph of the ad informs readers that Northwest "can offer something no other airline can: The knowledge, insight, and understanding that comes from more than 40 years of helping people do business in Asia." To top it off, the ad lists an 800 number through which customers can get a free booklet with more tips for doing business in the Far East.

   Another classic example of how advertising can be used as a customer education vehicle is a series of ads sponsored by The Machira Group, a Chicago-area stock brokerage firm. The Group's initial goal in advertising was to overcome the negative perceptions investors have of the brokerage industry. As a 1989 *Wall Street Journal* study pointed out, most individual investors do not have confidence in a broker's recommendations. This lack of faith comes largely from the fact that brokers earn their living by commissioned sales.

To rebuild confidence, the Machira Group decided to break with tradition and link the way it is paid to its performance. Instead of ads with animals and contrived slogans, the Machira campaign is educational, explaining the "pay for performance" issue. The firm's ads deal with the "real life" perceptions that investors have of stock brokers, and focus on Machira's unique philosophy. The aim is not to make quick sales but to attract potential investors who are looking for solid long-term results and who seek a high confidence level from a brokerage firm.

3. *Issue technical bulletins, newsletters, or other information-rich publications.* In Chapter 5, we discussed the newsletter issue at length. Now, let's reaffirm the power of the newsletter as an educational tool. Graham Communications provides customers and prospects with *Good Impressions*, a quarterly newsletter that deals with public relations, advertising, and marketing issues.

Written by Graham Communications staff, the newsletter's goal is to provide assistance to readers in dealing with marketing issues. It also aims at raising the level of understanding of what marketing is all about and how it contributes to a company's profitability. By sharing its experience with others, Graham Communications builds credibility and confidence. In fact, more than 50 percent of all the company's new business comes from readers of *Good Impressions*. That's not surprising to us. That's the real payoff from a customer education campaign.

In some industries, customer education publications have become essential for survival. Take the microcomputer field, where all the major players have developed publications that convey technical information, tricks of the trade, and suggestions for getting the most out of their software programs.

Microsoft Corporation, for example, has created a useful newsletter *Excellence* that provides invaluable tips for users of its word processing and spreadsheet programs. Lotus Development Corporation has broken ground with its slick full-color magazine called *Lotus*. Each issue is jam-packed with substantial articles aimed at helping novices and experts alike.

Both the Microsoft and Lotus publications do an excellent job of educating customers about ways to improve their productivity and enhance their knowledge of microcomputing. Their focus is on the end user's needs, not the companies' needs to sell more products. As a result, they do an excellent job of proving that both software giants have a great deal to offer users, and that they are committed to finding new solutions to old customer problems.

THE CHALLENGE AHEAD

Education as marketing creates a situation in which the salesperson can give extensive support, and conditions are created that serve as a positive environment for sales negotiations. In effect, it is much easier for salespersons to sell themselves when they are known as keepers of beneficial information.

Nevertheless, education as marketing demands a great deal of effort and more customer concern from a company and its people. Sales personnel must be more analytical in understanding customer needs. They must make a serious commitment to "getting inside the heads" of their customers and prospects. They can't push products. And there's no room for clever sales techniques or gimmicks. In short, salespeople must adopt a new style when doing business.

Finally, education as marketing also requires a great deal of patience. The seeds sown today may not bring results for weeks and months, sometimes even years. With customer education, effective communication becomes more important than ever. In addition, the ability to understand customer issues, to analyze problems, and to bring to bear solid information will be the salesperson's primary role.

A lot of work? Yes, but the rewards are well worth the extra effort. Bringing a company's expertise and experience to bear on problems faced by customers serves to elevate the business in the eyes of customers. An active "education-as-marketing" program will also constantly identify new prospects who can become exposed to the company's message. And that's both the task and the goal: keeping the pipeline filled with potential customers who are drawn ever closer to your company.

———— ✧ ————

Playing for Keeps

How to Generate Total Customer Loyalty

Graham's Law: If you're not cultivating present customers, you're not growing your company.

THE HARD FACTS OF BUSINESS

American business seems to espouse an interesting philosophy: "Find 'em, sell 'em, forget 'em." Whether it's a Fortune 500 firm or a local supplier, this attitude permeates business today. We once conducted an informal audit of the vendors with whom we do business during the year. We wanted to know:

- How many only came when they had something to sell?

- Which ones made contact only when a new salesperson was assigned to our territory?

- Did any stay in touch regularly to see if we needed their help?

- Was any specific effort made to cultivate our firm as a continuing customer?

Whether the vendor sold office supplies or computers, the answer was a resounding "no." We were so appalled by the results that we asked business associates and clients to evaluate our conclusions. The reactions were exactly the same! "Once they sell you something, they drop you like a hot potato until the next time." That was the unanimous conclusion.

Not only is this a sad commentary on the business community, but it appears to reflect a predominant sales strategy that focuses total attention on getting new customers rather than developing business from existing ones. In the same way, there is a trend among salespeople to expect customers to stop everything and demonstrate an inordinate interest in what the salesperson wants to sell. In doing so, salespersons communicate their message: Making the sale is all that's important.

If the behavior of salespeople betrays their words, then all the talk about "consultative" and "problem-solving" selling, as well as "quality service" is just that. A lot of talk. Of course, there are those who deny these charges, but the perceptions are there, nevertheless. And, if this is how customers perceive the sales process today, then that is the prevailing reality—no matter what claims are made to the contrary.

One of the primary goals of any company is to get existing customers to come back again and again and again. Sure, everyone wants new business, but to ignore existing customers is ultimately self-defeating and subversive to a company's overall, continued success. Besides, it's been shown time after time that the cost of attracting new customers far exceeds that of keeping old ones.

Today, retaining customers is more pertinent than ever because of changes in buying patterns. There is far less brand and vendor loyalty than in the past—more people are shopping around for the bottom line. We believe most of this is due to very poor customer relations, a failure to build an enduring bond with those whom we depend upon to buy our products and services.

In the same way, looking for the lowest price may be more a reflection of vendor dissatisfaction than a desire to get a rock-bottom deal. In effect, both the consumer and business buyers are far more skeptical than they were some years ago. When customers move from one vendor to another, they are looking for someone who will relate to them over a period of time and not just at the point of the sale. As a result, the consistent, effective cultivation of present customers is one of the best ways to increase sales over a period of time. It's the wise CEO or sales manager who understands this issue.

Whenever someone says, "We've got to increase sales," you can be sure there are problems. The sales "push" is the direct result of refusing to take the time and effort to create a climate so that customers will keep coming back. What can be done so existing customers will remain loyal and will actually want to continue to do business with you? There are basically two tactics you can use to ensure a long-term customer relationship: add value and target your satisfied customers.

ADDING VALUE

These days we hear the phrase "value added" bandied about quite a bit. Yet what does that really mean? For some, it's nothing but a slogan for attracting customers. In reality, adding value is a way of refocusing the business relationship. Instead of centering total attention on price, adding value allows customers to choose your firm for a variety of important reasons. More than anything else, adding value is a way of continually evaluating how much time you spend walking in your customers' shoes. Here are nine proven ways to add value to your marketing efforts.

1. *Think like a customer or client.* Consider your products and services in the broadest possible context, from "cradle to grave"—from the moment a customer decides to buy, to the moment he or she needs to discard or discontinue the service. Are there features or modifications that would make your goods or services more attractive to potential buyers? Are there aspects that enhance its utility?

2. *Give your products and services a special name.* Customers want to feel that they are getting something special. You can give it to them by developing product names for your product and service lines. If you do, you will be perceived as an innovator who occupies a unique position in the marketplace.

3. *Create a guarantee.* When you use a guarantee, you are sending the message that you have confidence in what you do or what you sell. Yes, guarantees can be dangerous. Yet, if you are unwilling to go out on a

limb for customers, how can you expect them to see your company as distinct from the competition? At some point, it is essential to put your business services or products on the line. A guarantee is the best way to do this.

4. *Let your customers know why they are smart to do business with you.* Customers want to feel that they have made a good decision when they choose you and your products or services. The most important continuing task is to reinforce that decision over a period of time. If you do, then your competition won't have a chance! And it's also easy to do.

   For example, if an article is published about your company, send a copy to your customers. If your products get an outstanding evaluation or review, make sure that information is sent to your customers. If you let doubts creep into a customer's mind, that is the beginning of the end.

5. *Give your customers ideas on how to improve their business operations.* Salespeople almost always miss an extraordinary opportunity. During their various dealings with a wide variety of businesses, they pick up ideas and techniques that can be helpful to their other customers. We're not talking about disclosing "trade secrets" or "proprietary information." But it's great to pass along helpful time-saving suggestions. "Over at the XYZ Company, they solved this same problem. Why don't you give them a call?" Customers appreciate this type of concern. And, it will mean more business for you.

6. *Say "Thank You" regularly.* Nothing is more important than saying "thank you." A call after a sale just to express your appreciation shows that you care about building a relationship. A simple hand-written note to the effect of "It was a year ago you bought a Model 200

from us and I appreciate your business" only takes a few minutes to write, but the customer reaction is impressive. If you receive a referral, make certain you thank the customer. At Graham Communications, we use gift certificates for personalized signature coffee mugs as a way of expressing our appreciation.

7. *Project a leadership image for your company.* All of us want to be with winners. In fact, we almost automatically shy away from people and companies that look like losers. This is almost an instinctive human reaction. That's why logos and printed materials are so important. In other words, make sure your firm has a distinctive "custom look," one that separates it clearly from other businesses in the same field. Work to qualify for awards for your company. This helps you stand out in the crowd. Or, keep customers informed about business trends. This places you out in front of the pack.

8. *Show a continuing interest in your customers.* This is actually easier said than done—it's a lot of work to keep a mailing list up-to-date. But constant communication indicates that you care about those who have chosen to do business with you. Mail copies of articles you think may be of interest to a customer. Then, when the time comes to make a sale, you have a reservoir of good will to draw upon. Also, send out reminders: "You may want to check your supply" or "Last year at this time you ordered...." By taking these simple steps, customers will come to rely on you.

9. *Ask your customers for their opinions.* The finest form of flattery is: "What do you think?" Those words show you value a person's ideas. This is how relationships that last year after year are made. Sure, you can hand out tickets to a show or a sports event, but the effect is not nearly as strong as getting someone to express his or her views.

129

Most people do not have many chances to talk about their ideas, so anyone who creates an opportunity for us to share our opinions makes a friend. That's the type of relationship we should build with our customers.

These simple, but effective, techniques will encourage present customers to keep coming back for more. Making an investment in building a bond with customers should be at the top of the list for a company that wants to succeed. Customer loyalty is also strategically critical; in the final analysis, what is more important than knowing your customers will be there when you need them next week, next month, or next year?

Now let's turn our attention to an essential, but often overlooked aspect of customer retention: focusing on satisfied customers.

BEYOND THE DISSATISFIED CUSTOMER

"Look for the unhappy customers," advises the sales manager. "Find the guy who's upset with his present supplier and you have a new customer." Locating the dissatisfied customer is the goal of every salesperson. It's spotting the crack in the armor, finding the soft underside of the belly that drives the sales enterprise forward every day of the week. Just get the door open a crack and we'll get through!

While salespeople are running around looking for the disgruntled customer, many companies are working hard to improve their quality of service. And their often intense efforts are now showing signs of paying major dividends. Of course, there are still valid, legitimate reasons for dissatisfaction, including unnecessary delivery delays, inaccurate orders, and high prices. At the same time, we can expect service from cutting edge companies to improve even more rapidly in the next few years.

Because of better service, it is going to be much more difficult to profit from the other guy's goofs. Yet, this does not mean all those satisfied customers should be avoided simply because they tell us, "Frankly, I am very happy with my current supplier. I have no reason to make a change."

IN SEARCH OF THE SATISFIED CUSTOMER

Contrary to the popular wisdom, it is the satisfied customers who the really good salesperson should be cultivating. Think about it for a minute. These customers are loyal to their suppliers. They don't make capricious changes. They respect those who call upon them and they appreciate the benefits of continuing relationships. They know they can count on the salesperson to come through in an emergency.

It's the dissatisfied customers who can be the real problem. Let the smallest thing go wrong and they look for a new vendor. There's no loyalty—it's only what you're going to do tomorrow that counts. So the real prize is selling the satisfied customers. Sure, it's the toughest sell. At the same time, these are the people and companies you should pursue because they are the customers who will stay with you over the long haul.

Unfortunately, many salespeople believe that the only way to get business from satisfied customers is to tantalize them with the lowest possible price. "Our prices are too high," salespeople whine to their sales managers. "They'll never give us their business."

Right—and wrong! Loyal business people are not seduced by price ploys. They know the game. Take a loss to get the business and then jack up the rate downstream. Satisfied customers have seen it hundreds of times. The price game is the wrong one to play with these people. In fact, selling the satisfied customer takes a lot more than a bag of old tricks. It requires a highly professional sales approach that incorporates a well-developed cultivation program.

The first step in using such a program is to identify the satisfied customers. This can be done by compiling a "druthers list"—the companies you would like to do business with in an ideal world. This list should be formalized and grow day by day because it is the "pot of gold" for the professional salesperson. It is from this vein that the real riches of sales can be mined.

Now that you know who your prospects are, you can begin your cultivation strategy. This is not a short-term or "knock 'em dead" project in which you try to take business away from your competitor. Rather, you abide by a fundamental fact about the contented customer: they don't want any dramatic changes. Rather, your goal is to establish just the right conditions so that your prospect will want to do business with you. You're not trying to sell your product or service, but to sell yourself and your company. In other words, your investment of time and effort is aimed at achieving credibility in the eyes of the satisfied customer.

Here are a few examples of how Graham Communications reaches the satisfied customers. Each time we complete a new brochure or other publication for a client, we have an overrun of several hundred copies. Then, we write a personal letter to everyone on our customer and "druthers" list and send it along with a copy of the brochure. In the letter we talk about how pleased we are to serve our clients and be involved with this particular project. Our goal is to show exciting ideas and new ways to communicate and to impress the readers with the fact that fine companies have chosen us to handle their marketing projects.

Our letter is free of phrases like "call us if you would like to get together about a program for your company." There's no telephone follow up. We're planting seeds and nurturing the young plants and we're willing to wait for just the right moment. At the same time, our quarterly newsletter is mailed to everyone on our customer and prospect list. It's designed to be educational and help readers come to the conclusion that our company is committed to solid, creative thinking.

Over a period of time, our "druthers" prospects—as well as our clients—are contacted through an array of carefully planned activities. We believe there's nothing wrong with making courtesy calls, as long as the goal is to make our company familiar to our prospects. We make an effort to discover everything we can about the business. Then, from time to time, we offer helpful suggestions, new ideas, and beneficial comments.

You, too, can pursue a similar course. When you do get around to contacting people on your druthers list, find opportunities for giving away samples. Perform a service without charge. And, at the right time, suggest a no obligation, free trial. Throughout the program, don't try to manipulate the prospect—only an inexperienced salesperson would take such a tact. Rather, work on fashioning a very precise picture in your "satisfied customer's" mind, one that will emerge slowly. Remember, you're making an investment in your prospect and it shouldn't be rushed.

Throughout this highly crafted process, you are very deliberately and carefully separating yourself from the competition. You cannot know when your "satisfied customer" will emerge into a live prospect, although the time will come. Not with each and every one on your list, of course. But, at some point, there will be a problem. That's when your prospect will come looking for you. There will be an emergency and your telephone will ring. The prospect will be staring at a vacuum and you will be asked to fill the void.

Selling the satisfied customer is a process. It's a matter of turning the tables, of establishing all the right conditions so that the business comes to you. Of course, there will be those who find all this too complicated and time consuming. They want to go out and get the order now. That may make for limited short-term success. Yet, when your "satisfied customer development program" is implemented on a continuing basis, you'll discover that so much business will be coming your way the orders will take care of themselves. Most important, once you've won the hearts and wallets of a satisfied customer, chances are that you'll have a long-term source of revenue.

CUSTOMER SERVICE: AN OUNCE OF PREVENTION

The best laid plans for retaining customers will fail if you can't provide a level of customer service that generates deep bonds of loyalty. That means a great deal more than offering an 800 number or teaching people to answer the phone with a cheery tone. It means getting employees to reverse their roles and begin *thinking* like customers.

A good place to start is to get employees to consider their language. Thought and language mirror each other, and when the right words are used, the organization begins to behave as if they were true. Use the wrong words and the opposite happens.

Here are some words for inspiring customer confidence and, at the same time, influencing an organization's behavior toward improved service:

1. *"I'll take care of that for you."* Wherever a problem lands first is the only place for it to be solved. The words used must be simple and direct. When this happens employees feel a greater sense of worth. They see themselves as important because the words empower them to act. They are not just endless links in a never-ending chain; rather, they are significant individuals who have the ability to make a difference.

2. *"I take full responsibility."* Can you remember when you last heard these words? When managers, by their actions, continually protect themselves from criticism, you can be certain no one else in the organization is about to take any responsibility.

   Yet, employees will move heaven and earth when they have told customers "I'll take full responsibility."

If there's a mistake, let's admit it. By taking responsibility we get to solutions—and customer satisfaction.

3. *"We want your business."* Why should we ever assume that customers know that we want their business unless we tell them? Remember the librarian who said it would be easy to keep all the books in place if people didn't use them? Well, too many businesses convey the impression that customers are an interference. When someone hears, "We want your business," it is clear that the customer counts.

4. *"Thank you for thinking of us."* This short sentence is what business is all about. When you walk into a store to make a purchase, you are in a very real sense paying a compliment to that business. Those who work for the company will better understand this relationship when they say, "Thank you for thinking of us." Everyone feels good—the one giving the compliment and the one receiving it.

5. *"Consider it done."* These are the magic words in business. They make more sales than all the training programs in the world. They keep customers coming back. They set a company apart from all competition.

Every business has only one reason for existing: to make something happen for customers, on time. That's what business is all about. Customers want to be reassured that you will do what needs to be done, not that you'll "try your best." "Consider it done" makes the person saying the words feel in charge and the customer is left with the assurance of being in good hands.

There is only one goal when it comes to service: to instill confidence in the customer. And words work wonders. They establish positive relationships. They create confidence. Most important, they keep customers coming back. Use these key words and phrases and you know you'll be in business for a long, long time.

In addition to the obvious value of repeat business, the underlying mechanism, customer loyalty, is a very important strategic tool. When customers feel a deep sense of loyalty, in effect they insulate themselves, from your competitors. By striving for total loyalty, you are thus making a bold competitive maneuver—without firing a shot. As marketing people lay the groundwork for using loyalty as a competitive tool, your salespeople must do their share in making your company the long-term vendor of choice. In Chapter 10 we'll examine a special application of this principle: using magnet marketing in the professional services.

Chapter
TEN

———— ✧ ————

Marketing
Professional Services

How to Cultivate New
Clients and Retain Old
Ones

Graham's Law: You may not be a box of soap,
but your packaging is still important.

Just about every industry has learned how to grow—and sometimes even survive—by harnessing the principles of effective marketing. Yet, there's a segment of the business world that is still unsure of itself when it comes to marketing: Professional Services.

Lawyers, CPA firms, dentists, insurance agents, physicians, financial planners, architects, and others who view themselves as the elite of the business community shy away from a strong embrace of the marketplace. There are exceptions, of course. Within the legal profession, for example, some personal injury practitioners are advertising boldly and achieving impressive results in many instances. Some of these lawyers have even closed the doors of their posh high rise offices and hung out their shingles on storefronts and in shopping malls in order to be more highly visible to their prospective clients.

Still, for the most part, the professional services industry continues to debate "the ethics of marketing"—sometimes endlessly! Perhaps these professionals see themselves as "different" from other business people. Or maybe the problem results from the fact that many professionals do not really see themselves as business people at all. Perhaps it is this "we're a little above everyone else" attitude that causes them so much discomfort whenever the idea of marketing professional services is discussed. Whatever the reason, the "we're different" posture is keeping many from achieving optimum growth.

Even though some professionals persist in mouthing rather self-righteous excuses for avoiding effective marketing, more than anything else, marketing was made for professional services. The goal of marketing is to get the client to come to you. That's what the "Yellow Pages" are all about. It is what makes word of mouth so powerful. Good marketing harnesses and accelerates the process so that word of mouth works more efficiently and faster. A marketing program enables a professional to pull more clients to come through the door on a regular basis.

The key to professional services marketing is the same as marketing anything else: In order to get more business, you must be the first in mind when the client has a problem or when the prospect is ready. A corollary goes like this: If you market your services properly, you are making the prospective client aware of the possibility that an *unperceived* problem exists and that you can solve it.

An effective professional services marketing program will achieve very specific goals:

1. *Pre-establish a relationship with the prospect.* Actually, this is what word of mouth is all about. Referrals are not based on someone making a detailed inquiry into your competence. Quite the contrary, studies show that choosing a lawyer or doctor or CPA is a low involvement decision.

   If someone says: "I know a great CPA firm," that's recommendation enough for most people. The question of whether or not your firm has the necessary expertise is not even an issue. How many times do people call a lawyer to do collections without even asking if the firm specializes in this field? The fact of the matter is that most people choose professional services without doing any research.

   If you make the effort to build a pre-established relationship, you will become the preferred professional or the professional of choice when the need for your service arises. You will get the call. Your firm will be chosen simply because you have given the person permission to contact you.

2. *Create the perception that you're the expert in your field.* This is where marketing can be an extremely powerful competitive weapon. If you are to be highly successful, you must be perceived as a leading expert. You may have the education and knowledge, and you may even be recog-

nized by your peers as the best in your field. But unless your competence is recognized by those who can benefit from your services, your potential will be limited.

3. *To converse with many prospects at the same time.* Instead of spending four hours on the golf course with one prospect, marketing lets you take your message to a much wider audience. That's what makes it cost effective.

   Even more important, your conversation with prospects is non-threatening. Effective marketing is really an education process. If prospects learn from you, they are listening. And that's what you want to achieve. Only when the people receiving the message are comfortable will they be receptive.

   Conversely when people feel threatened, they run away—just look at how the world perceives insurance agents. Instead of taking time to communicate their message, insurance agents always seem to be in an overly aggressive sales mode. No wonder we all groan and take cover when we see the friendly insurance agent coming toward us. The smart agents have learned to market their services to the public so that people want to do business with them.

Whether you're dealing with a prospect or an existing client, the goal is to be perceived as the professional of choice. Think for a moment about the words we use. We like to openly talk about "my doctor," "my lawyer," and "my accountant"— even "my psychiatrist" today. We're proud of the fact that we have made what we consider to be "the right choice."

To sum up, marketing helps cement the client relationship. That's essential because professional relationships are far more vulnerable than they were in times past. No longer does a company necessarily keep the same accounting firm for decades. A similar problem exists for all other professionals including doctors, lawyers, and insurance agents. In order to retain business, the client must feel that you are the right person or firm for the job.

The quality of your work is important, of course. But, as we all know, competence alone is not enough. Marketing is a way to communicate the idea that choosing you is a wise decision. Unless the relationship with your clients is reinforced over and over again, the client will eventually make a change.

CLIENT CULTIVATION TIPS FOR PROFESSIONALS

Now that you realize the value of marketing your professional services firm, consider the following techniques for bringing in new clients and retaining old ones:

1. *Develop and maintain a good mailing list.* The most critical element in any marketing program is a mailing list. Yet, more often than not, this is given a low priority, or totally neglected.

   Your mailing list should contain information on past clients (yes, you have lost some over the years), present clients, and—most important—prospects. Whenever professionals hear the word "prospect," they begin to squirm. Yet, if your marketing program is truly educational and, therefore, beneficial, you should be eager to include on your mailing list anyone you honestly believe can be helped by your service. Nevertheless, even the best mailing list is worthless unless it is used regularly.

2. *Publish a newsletter.* Although just about every business can benefit from having a newsletter (see Chapter 5), it is professionals who can get the most from pub-

lishing a regular newsletter. In fact, no professional firm should be without its own newsletter. If a "canned" newsletter is the best that your accounting or insurance firm can do, go with it. But a newsletter that you develop in-house will probably have the greatest impact.

3. *Write and submit bylined articles.* As we explained in Chapter 6, a bylined article is one that appears in a publication and has your name on it as the author. No matter who you serve or what your specialty happens to be, there are ample opportunities to have articles published in newspapers, magazines, and newsletters that your potential clients will likely read. Of course, it takes time and some talent to write articles that editors are willing to publish. You may have the ideas, but they must be expressed in a way that is appropriate for the reader.

   Once published, bylined articles can work even harder for you if you have them reprinted and sent to both current clients and prospects. (Now you can see why a good mailing list is the linchpin of any marketing program.) Published articles are also very effective when included in presentations, because they enhance your credibility.

4. *Don't be afraid of advertising.* Advertising is nothing more than telling your story the way you want to tell it, where you want to tell it, and when. Nevertheless, the question persists: Should professionals advertise? In two words: You bet!

   With the right message in the right publications, you present yourself as a leading contender in your field (see Chapter 7 for more details). Of course, advertising costs money. In fact, advertising can be downright expensive. But over a period of time, advertising will establish you as a leader in your field and bring you the inquiries that open the door to more presentations or consultations. And, the more presentations you make, the more business you'll develop.

What should you expect from an ad? If you sit around and wait for the telephone to ring every time an ad runs, you'll do exactly what so many others have done who are uninformed—stop advertising. To succeed with advertising, make sure you:

- *Write the ad from the prospect's viewpoint.* Unless the ad says what the person reading it wants to hear, you're wasting your money.
- *Make an offer.* We recommend using what we call "the marketing pamphlet." This is a small folder with a title something like this: **Twelve Questions You Should Ask Before Choosing An Accounting Firm.** Offer the pamphlet free for the asking. Why? Because this is a way to develop leads. Add the names to your mailing list after you've sent a personal letter to accompany the pamphlet. Anyone asking for this type of brochure is a prospect!

When these marketing techniques are included in an overall plan so that the marketing effort is both consistent and unified, they bring clients to your firm's door.

Today, the marketing of professional services is no longer a luxury or an option merely to be tolerated or ignored. Marketing is a necessity if you want to build a stronger professional practice with some assurance of longevity.

Even more important, an effective marketing program allows you to do what you do best: provide quality service to your clients because you are not wasting your time trying to develop new business in nonproductive ways.

Chapter
E L E V E N

◇

Surviving Through Marketing

How to Make Your Sales Go Up When the Economy Goes Down

Graham's Law: There's only one valid assumption in business: The road ahead is always uphill.

P.S. PLEASE HELP ME

"Could you come right over?" Ad agencies and PR firms hear those words several times a month. Without exception, the caller has a problem—often a serious one. Over a period of time, sales have either leveled off or taken a nosedive. Finally, and almost in desperation, they realize it's time to take action.

So the client calls a meeting, and more often than not, the opening sentence will be: "I've been thinking about doing some promotion for a long time and I want to get going." A little later, the truth comes out. "We're in trouble...."

At the first signs of weakening sales or a downturn in the economy, the management of most businesses gets scared. Then, with a terminal case of jittery nerves derailing their logic, they mobilize their forces and rally for increased sales. At the same time, they shoot themselves in the foot by taking away the marketing tools so vital to survival. In other words, they signal full speed ahead by going into reverse!

Underneath their macho masks, too many business leaders lack confidence in their ability to deal with the difficult issues of a troubled or flat economy. They see themselves as "tough minded," but, in reality, they behave like tenderfoots. Although they talk about "a level playing field," what they really want is a downhill run.

Those who make it successfully through the problem periods think differently because they arm themselves with the techniques of "Survival Marketing." They know how to make sales go up when the economy goes down.

In the down times, the wise business person doesn't panic or give in to unwarranted fear. Instead of taking a defensive posture, he goes on the offensive. He doesn't pull back, because he knows how customers think: The time to get the lowest price is when a supplier feels threatened and his back is against the wall. At the first signs of fear, that's the moment to drive the hardest deal. The good news is that you don't have to stand for that kind of cutthroat treatment!

The techniques of "Survival Marketing" are very easy to use, and they begin with a simple, yet very powerful concept: concentrate on the basics. Your company's single most important job is to get and keep customers. The only way of doing this is to help your customers solve their problems better than anyone else! Don't assume you have the answers. Learn what each customer means by "better." Then, adapt your product or service so that it is perceived as "better" in the eyes of your customers and prospects.

The customer relationship is always much more fragile than we like to think. In fact, customer satisfaction depends on just one issue: Meeting needs on time, every time. Work harder than ever to meet as many of those needs as you can. Concentrate on consulting and tailor your services to meet precise needs. This means taking more time to be helpful, understanding, and supportive of your customers.

It is, therefore, important during tough times to make sure it's your customers who are running your business. A marketing-driven company operates just one way: The total effort—product, service, price, and promotion—must be adapted to the needs and wants of customers.

Finally, think like a customer to discover what you can do to bring out your uniqueness. Remember, though, it's never the *value you want to add* that makes the difference, it's the *value the customer wants to receive* that's important.

In addition to working on business basics, think about these other survival measures for turning adversity into success the next time you feel the "weight of the elephant upon your chest":

1. *Focus all your attention and energy on your customers.* Make this one an ironclad rule and never forget it. When things go *soft*, everyone around you will want to

spend time talking about problems with the competition—better products, lower prices, more visibility in the marketplace. Once this gets started, it will sweep through your company like a death-dealing virus. Sales will drop further because now there's a scapegoat. Don't bow to the temptation of listening to what are nothing more than excuses for poor performance. Focus constantly on what needs to be done to create more and more customers.

2. *Work especially hard at retaining present customers.* Even if customers are spending less, don't let them be tempted to take their business elsewhere. It costs so much more to gain a new customer than it does to keep an old one.

3. *Build your prospect list.* Put some quality time into developing your "druthers list," as we described earlier. If you had your druthers, what two or three hundred firms would you like to do business with? Now, make regular contact with these companies. Explain why you have a special interest in them. Show how dealing with you has special benefits for them. Make your goal clear: Ask what you will have to do to get their business.

4. *Don't waste your time on deadbeats.* In tough times, it's easy to get victimized by the worst prospective customers. They'll be out in force, just waiting for you. They'll suck up your time and never give you an order. Therefore, never give a quote or a proposal to anyone who makes either of these comments: "Price is not an object" or "We buy on price alone." No one needs losers and this crowd is all losers! Now that you know how to recognize the "bad guys," go after the rest.

5. *Increase your presence in the marketplace.* Ideally, a marketing program should be consistent throughout the

year in order to get rid of the valleys and establish an overall upward growth pattern. Still, during downturns, companies tend to cut off marketing funds and focus on essential expenditures. But what could be more essential then ensuring a steady flow of orders? A McGraw-Hill Research analysis of 600 industrial firms shows that companies maintaining or increasing advertising during the 1981–1982 recession averaged higher sales during that period and for the following three years than companies that cut advertising.

Clearly, if you want the business, then it is essential to be the leader. Even if you occupy a narrow niche, make sure you're perceived as the dominant force. The faster you take the initiative during tough times, the better. Flood the marketplace with your presence through a carefully calculated program of advertising, direct mail, and public relations.

Also, become more aggressive. Change your marketing strategy to fit the psychology of the times. Emphasize how your products or services save time, cut costs, and increase productivity. If you take this route, you'll stand out in the marketplace because most of your competitors will pull back to a more-defensive protective position.

6. *Maintain a strong financial position.* Keep your bank informed about your business. Is your line of credit intact? Although you pay close attention to the accounts receivable, watch for *slow pay* trends and take action fast. And, of course, take advantage of every possible discount for prompt payment.

7. *Keep a watchful eye on the competition.* Don't assume your competitors are sleeping. They may be making moves that could cut into your customer base. More than ever it's important to scout the competition.

8. *Practice niche marketing.* Look for those markets that best match your company's products and service—and come out swinging. Strive to become the big fish in a small pond. Chances are competition is less intense in these markets and your strong position will fend off unwanted intruders. As you successfully serve new customers, you have a good chance to become a preferred supplier.

9. *Polish up your company image.* Make sure your firm is perceived in the best light by customers, prospects, suppliers, and opinion leaders in your business and the community at large. Does your company appear professional? Capable? Is customer service your number one priority? Then publicize those special qualities that make you more professional than your competitors.

10. *Make your employees and suppliers your firm's ambassadors.* Tough times can cause anxiety. Don't let it show. Negative messages spread like wildfire and can hurt your image with employees, suppliers, and customers. Emphasize good news via pay envelope stuffers, bulletins, and newsletters. Don't ever fake it, but always accentuate the positive.

11. *Dramatize your business.* In troubled times, businesses tend to become bland and dull. This merely compounds the problem. Excitement sells. Far too many management people tend to have arrived at the top by bleeding themselves dry of innovative thinking. Problem periods require extra flair, color, and imagination.

12. *Drag the top management out in the field.* American business has been subverted by a most destructive myth: When you get to the top, you can be insulated from the two essential elements of any business—employees and customers. The excitement created by customers seeing the president of the company will be so over-

whelming that sales will increase automatically. Remember, big offices are bad for business. The people who occupy them get too comfortable. Worse yet, they begin believing their own ideas. Drag management out into the field. That's the only place to play ball.

13. *Be daring.* Take a scenic trip inside the customer's head. When customers stop buying, it is time to change your thinking. No one cares what you want to sell. It is what the customer wants to buy that's important. It is so easy for us to get wrapped up in our own problems in periods of economic difficulty that we forget that our customers are facing many of the same obstacles. If you are not addressing those problems and finding solutions, then you don't deserve to make sales. Your job is to make your customer successful. When that happens, people buy. It sounds so simple, but most people in management miss the point.

14. *Stand firm.* The easiest way to get more business is to cut prices. In fact, if you cut them deep enough, you'll have more business than you can handle. You will also be bankrupt. Pricing problems are almost always the direct result of not having taken the time and effort to establish value in the mind of the customer.

    The "best price" and the "lowest price" are not synonymous terms, even though sales managers and sales personnel often confuse them. Your job is to educate every customer—particularly the tough ones— why you offer the "best price." Most likely, it will be some combination of reliability, quality, and service. That's what you're really selling.

15. *Assume that no one, including long-time customers, knows what you sell.* When all is well and sales roll in, we all get lax. We're so busy we forget about the basics. Has

anyone ever said to you, "All the years I've been doing business with you and I didn't know you sell an X, Y, or Z." If you're truthful, then you'll admit how often those words are spoken. What they reveal is a vast untapped resource of new sales. The people you do business with regularly will buy more from you if you only let them know how you can help them. The key to success here is endless repetition. Tell them over and over again—just keep repeating your story in new and interesting ways. Then ask yourself this question: "If even my best customers are ignorant of what we do, then what about everyone else?"

One company that doesn't leave anything to chance in this area is American Express. The Amex direct mail people know that staying in front of a customer is the only way to make a sale. You may not buy today, but you'll have another chance next month—or six months from now. When you're ready, an American Express catalog will be there.

16. *Stick to your knitting.* Success in difficult times comes about by staying on track. Whenever problems arise, we all look for scapegoats. The sales force is bad. The sales manager is tired. Production can't deliver on time. Quality is lousy. About that time, other scapegoats creep in. We have the wrong products. We're not offering the right services. We've got to make changes. Before long, we're doing anything and everything but what we do best. Don't let such distractions deter you. Stick with your knitting—you know what your company does best. Do it!

A good example of sticking to your knitting is A. G. Edwards & Sons, Inc., the century-old brokerage firm with some 300 offices across the country. Unlike so many other houses that accost customers with more products than a Sears catalog, A. G. Edwards continues to project a solid, clear message of professionalism, a message that should be attractive to those who are looking for an "old fashioned" stockbroker.

17. *Radiate confidence.* You may have the best products or services in the world, but that's not enough. Go the next step. Show enthusiasm by going out of your way to prove that you're service-oriented. And use the magic word, "Sure." Since we're all in the problem solving business, respond to requests with a strong affirmative. You may not have all the answers at the moment. That's not important. You can get them later. When you're talking to the customer, convey confidence and be 100% positive. It will get you more and more business.

A related concept is to let everyone know that you're in top fighting shape. Remember a fundamental principle: People want to do business with companies that are streamlined, focused, aggressive, and have goals. If you're nervous, cautious, and jittery, you'll telegraph your anxieties to your customers. Then you'll really be in trouble! Market your message that you're different from everyone else on the street. Look different. Act different. Get your blood moving! It will get you the business you want because you'll deserve it.

"Survival Marketing" is neither a gimmick nor something new. It's just plain good, solid marketing sense, based on the fundamental assumption that tough times don't last—tough people do. When you get tough with yourself and your business, success is on the way. That applies to good times and tough times alike.

Only the tough-minded dare to practice "Survival Marketing" as a regular course of action. Long ago, they discovered the most basic of all ideas in business: The primary goal is not to make sales, but to make customers. That's the goal of "Survival Marketing." That's how you stay in business regardless of the state of the economy or the competitive scene.

Finally, smart business people never get complacent. When revenues are up, they think as if disaster were lurking around the corner. They recognize that suvival marketing tactics should be deployed every day of the year. They strive to position their companies so well in the mind of prospects that when the time comes for the buying decision, their firm is the only choice. By making an appropriate investment in customer cultivation during good and bad times alike, they maximize their chances of continuous smooth success in an ever-changing and sometimes tumultuous marketplace.

❖

Understanding the Sales Process

Overcoming Common Sales Problems

Graham's Law: Absolutely nothing sells itself.

OF PARTS AND WHOLES

The ancient Chinese saw the world in terms of "complementary opposites" called yin and yang. Yin things, like night and females of a species, we're the opposite, but complement of yang things, like day and males of a species. In the same way, marketing and sales are like yin and yang—two sides of the same coin.

The best magnet marketing program in the world will do you little good if it isn't complemented by a strong sales effort. Unfortunately, the state of sales these days leaves much to be desired. In this chapter, we'll take a look at the three problems underlying the difficulties with sales. The first concerns the basic mind-set of today's salespeople. The second focuses on problems within the company itself, the sales environment. The third concerns that myth of the sales personality, which too often drives away potentially excellent salespeople. In Chapter 13 we'll go on to explore some of the solutions to these problems.

THE MENTAL SALES KILLERS

It's easy to find books, audio cassettes, and video tapes that explain the secret of selling. But learning how sales get killed is just as important as how to make more sales. Most salespeople avoid the topic, because they are basically optimistic, nothing-can-keep-me-down folks who have a strong tendency to avoid anything that's viewed as negative.

In reality, though, even the most positive, enthusiastic sales professional tends to develop attitudes and behavior patterns that can reduce success and destroy sales. We have identified eight sales killers—assumptions or attitudes that can greatly reduce a salesperson's effectiveness. Each one develops slowly, but becomes a fixed pattern. By giving a serious review to your own practices as a salesperson, you can discover whether or not any of these killers are keeping you from reaching the top.

159

1. *I know more than my customers.* Because salespeople are in fact the experts on what they sell, it is easy to assume that they know more than their customers. This is a very subtle sales killer because although salespeople do not intend to demean or talk down to a customer, to be successful they must be helpful. Their real goal is to pass along expertise. But that isn't the way it may come across to the people they deal with every day. Without even realizing it, they may be making their customers feel uncomfortable, ignorant—even inferior. This drives customers away and loses sales.

2. *My customers know more than I do.* This is the flip side of the preceding issue. For one reason or another, a salesperson may conclude that the customer has a lot more knowledge than he or she does. In fact, many times it is the customer who feels uneasy or even inadequate, but covers up the situation with a bravado that dupes the salesperson into believing that the customer is the expert. After all, isn't he the one who is actually operating the business? He knows what he needs. As a result of this facade, salespeople hold back and don't let the customer have the full benefit of their knowledge and experience. Which again leads to limited sales.

3. *There's no doubt about it. My customers think of me when a need arises.* This is a particularly insidious sales killer because it develops over a long period of time. In fact, most salespeople don't even feel the pain until long after this killer has struck.

   Once a salesperson has had particular customers for several years and has done a good job meeting their requirements, it is normal to assume that repeat business is in order. The account is "safe."

   No account is really safe, though. Everyone—including the customer—gets bored with business routines. We all like to inject a little novelty or excitement into our lives. We look for it. So even though a customer may be satisfied with a salesperson's performance, he may nevertheless start looking for something new and different. That's when competitors get their proverbial feet in the door. They may not give the customer a better product or even a lower price, but what they lay on the table appears to be different and exciting. And that's what gets the business.

4. *When there's a problem to be solved, my customers turn to me.* If you're a salesperson, there's often a very good reason to think that a customer will almost automatically turn to you when the need arises. You've been servicing the customer efficiently. You've always been helpful and accessible. Therefore, why shouldn't you expect the customer to ask you to help solve their problems?

   Despite your hard work, another sales killer is at work here. It's insidious and relentless. While you see yourself as a problem solver, your customer may view you as a "provider." "I just can't understand why they called in someone else," you say. "I've always been there when they needed me and I've never messed up an order." That's good—but it is not enough. It is important to project a strong, clear "problem solver" image and to reinforce continually the fact that you don't just get the job done right and on time, but that you are a valuable resource for your customers.

5. *Forget it. That outfit will never be anything but small change.* All of us develop the habit of "pegging" customers. We decide how much business they are going to be able to give us. We even tend to establish a "ceiling" for what we will make on their deals. Bingo! Believe it or not, we also convey this same "message" to our customers. They are

able to recognize how important (or, more likely, unimportant) we think they are to us. Eventually these customers will go elsewhere when they believe they are being treated as second-rate citizens.

6. *I've worked hard to make sure I'm "in solid" with my customers—nothing could cause them to make a change.* A great relationship with customers is a key to success in selling. At the same time, it's possible that some customers feel that the relationship is too close or even too strong. Although a salesperson doesn't take them for granted, they may feel he or she isn't working hard enough for them. They may even feel that the salesperson has come to count on their orders. Salespeople who think they're "in solid" with a particular customer should think about it from the customer's viewpoint. This sales killer has the power to destroy even the largest accounts!

7. *I know my customers trust me.* Just because customers are buying from you does not mean that they have confidence in you. This is perhaps the most lethal of all sales killers because we never know what's happening until it is too late. "I called on that company regularly. I gave them more attention than they really needed. I can't believe it. They always give the big orders to someone else."

    Why does this happen? It's beyond explanation. Or is it? In reality, customers "categorize" salespeople. They come to conclusions about their capabilities, knowledge, and ability to handle situations. Without realizing it, you may be projecting a "small order image." In other words, the customer believes that a salesperson has the ability to meet needs up to a certain level. Beyond that point, they exceed the customer's comfort level and the business goes elsewhere.

As surprising as it may seem, the reverse is true, too. You may not be getting the smaller orders simply because the customer doesn't feel you really want the business or that you'll give the smaller order the proper attention. In other words, that you're "big-order oriented." Either way, the sales killer strikes again.

8. *There's no question about it. A big sale is the best sale.* How could it be anything else? A big sale is obviously a good sale. We live and work for them. They're almost always a great test for our skills as salespeople. More than anything else, they are a personal barometer depicting clearly our level of achievement. The "big sale" lets us—and everyone else—know we are good, really good at what we do.

The huge orders make us feel that we're worth more money, too. That competitors would love to have us on their team. Maybe this is the problem. Big sales enhance our egos. They make us feel bigger than life. Nothing can stop us now. It's what they do for us that makes them so alluring, so attractive.

Nevertheless, "big sales" alone do not make great salespeople—except in our own minds. Anyone who has spent much time sitting on a stool with one leg knows how precarious a perch it really is. As the moments pass, all our effort goes into maintaining our balance. Why we're sitting on the stool is less and less important. Just trying to keep our balance is everything. Well, it's the same way in sales. The "big sale" can be a killer because all our attention is directed toward getting the account, leaving little or no energy—or desire—to foster the many other customers that go into making up a well-balanced book of accounts.

All this suggests that it is important to keep your mental antenna up and open at all times. A very high level of alertness is essential in sales. And it's not just for new opportunities, either. Sensitive salespeople are constantly evaluating themselves in the same way that their customers are evaluating them. They know that the products or services they offer are only one part of the selling equation. Although it's difficult, a certain amount of calculated detachment is important to their continued success.

Salespeople should therefore assess continually their relationship with customers. The best way to do this is to look at what's happening from the outside, as a third-party observer. Here are a few questions to ask yourself when you want to get a new perspective on your performance:

- How do my customers view me? Are my perceptions accurate or are they colored by my own thinking? Do I see what I want to see?

- Why am I important to my customers? What's the basis of our relationship? Has it changed over time? How did it start and what is it today? What should be changed?

- Have they pegged me? If so, where am I in their thinking? What can I do to alter their perceptions of me?

- What does my particular style say to my customers? What messages are coming across?

The more aware you are of how your customers see you, the more you will be able to adjust the way you deal with them and maximize your sales potential. Never forget that the eight sales killers are on the loose. They go with you every day, just waiting to cause problems and destroy your continued success. The killers never go away. But whether or not they are set free to attack is up to you.

THE AILING SALES ENVIRONMENT

Many companies think they're doing their salespeople a favor by "tuning them up"—sending them to seminars, plying them with all sorts and sizes of prizes and plaques. They pull, prod, push, and shove—just about anything imaginable to motivate their salespeople. The implication of all this is quite sinister: having the *right* attitude, the *right* presentation, and, of course, the *right* price makes sales. So by constantly refining and improving selling techniques, more sales will be made.

All this presents a picture of the salesperson as the center of attention. That's why every salesperson learns quickly to ask what is believed to be the critical question: "Am I talking to the decision maker?" One way or the other, sales is seen as a matter of persuading, impressing, influencing, and—to one degree or the other—manipulating the prospective buyer into saying "yes."

Even in so-called "non-manipulative selling," getting the order is still the goal. In the same way, we can talk all we want about the salesperson as "problem solver," yet when all the fancy and faddish terms are stripped away, the individual is measured in terms of meeting a sales quota.

So the central focus is the "selling situation." And that's the wrong place to start when it comes to building sales. Yet, this is the precise approach taken by most of the so-called leading sales experts today. The emphasis is always on selling and how to get the customer to behave in a way that gets the order.

Sadly, things could be very different, if only management realized that the *real* break for salespeople isn't better "training," a new bag of tricks, or more incentives—higher commission, "better" territories, new cars, bigger bonuses, or more clever contests. These are nothing more than pressure cooker schemes for masking the total absence of conditions that are conducive to buying. The fact is, whether they're inside or outside, salespeople need the only gift that makes a difference:

Customers who want to do business with them. All anyone in sales really wants is qualified customers so they can do what management expects them to do—make sales.

This sounds so simple and elementary, yet it's a point that most companies miss year after year. As a result, most salespeople start each day with two strikes against them.

The solution? As we've argued in this book, it's getting companies to focus on establishing the conditions for actually creating customers, of fostering an environment in which customers want to do business with your company. When that happens, salespeople are so busy they don't have time to complain.

Whether it makes a product or sells a service, a company's responsibility is to prepare the way so that customers already have a predisposition to buy, long before the salesperson arrives. Such a buying environment exists when a business takes the sales task so seriously that it is willing to invest the effort required to create a positive buying atmosphere for the salesperson. When a company accepts that its primary mission is to create customers, sales takes on a new dimension. Salespeople are free to focus on making the sale. They can answer questions about the company, the product, or the service, reaffirm what the customer already believes, demonstrate the appropriateness of the product or service for the customer's situation, or work out the terms. In other words, the salesperson can focus on putting the order together, not selling the customer.

To recap what needs to be done to create the kind of environment that will support sales, companies need to put into place a solid cultivation program that consists of three separate customer development stages:

1. *Customer Identification.* We've seen how most companies spend little time or effort in building a prospective customer base. From time to time, they "buy" mailing lists. But they do not maintain a regular program of

adding names to a prospective customer list. They simply do not know who their prospects are other than to say, "Everyone is a possible customer." That, of course, is nonsense and simply reflects a lack of understanding of who can benefit from the firm's products or services.

One of the chief marketing tasks is to undertake programs that result in the development of prospects. If new names are not being added to the company's list daily, there is no customer identification program.

With very few exceptions, our experience points out a major problem in the customer identification area. Simply put, most companies do not have effective procedures for specifically identifying potential customers. To make matters worse, far too few firms maintain existing and past customer lists, other than "sales records." In reality, these businesses are "working in the dark."

2. *Customer Cultivation.* The goal of marketing is to create the conditions for a sale to take place, to cultivate the customer. It is probably the most difficult for most companies simply because it demands continuous planning and strenuous effort in terms of consistent implementation. Yet, it is the heart of the sales process.

The goal of customer cultivation is to reinforce your reliability, creativity, responsiveness, and ability to meet the customer's needs. If you do it in enough ways over a period of time, you have developed a customer. The entire sales atmosphere is changed dramatically. At that point, the sales task is not one of negotiating price, but of negotiating the *process* by which the product or service will be delivered. This happens because the customer is already convinced and has "bought" your company.

3. *Customer Response.* Customer identification and customer cultivation have but one goal: Customer response. If you adopt the philosophy, "We only want to do business with those who want to do business with us," your marketing efforts will create an atmosphere that motivates businesses to seek your advice and counsel.

Here's just one example to describe what we are talking about when it comes to customer response. Over five years ago, we bought a telephone system for our offices. At that time, we added the name of the salesman to our mailing list. Four times a year, he received our newsletter. When he took on a new position with another company, the newsletter followed him. He realized the firm needed marketing services. When our newsletter arrived with an article called "The Ten Worst Marketing Mistakes," he sent it off to his sales manager who had the salesman arrange a meeting with us. The result was a series of meetings, a proposal, and an action plan. And, finally, we won the account.

All this is not a shift in tactics when it comes to sales. It represents a totally different strategy aimed at achieving long-term results. Why not get the most from a sales force by giving them an environment in which they can best use their skills? Why make your salespeople spend their precious time in front of customers trying to get over hurdles that should have been removed well before they walked through the door? Give a salesperson a buying environment and watch the figures climb off the charts.

THE MYTH OF THE SALES PERSONALITY

The tragedy of sales is simply that many good people never choose a sales career. They're frightened off by myths that cause them to run whenever someone says, "You ought to be in sales." Others never even entertain the idea of sales because of a negative image they have of the field.

As a result, companies suffer and so do their sales. Many of those who are attracted to sales come in to the field because they lack the skills or education to pursue other careers. The lure of "making it big" appeals to the person who is always looking for the quick and easy way. Just look at most of the ads under the heading "sales help wanted" in a Sunday newspaper. "Earn $100K your first year" or "Make your dreams come true," the ads promise. In order to attract the gullible, the ads make it clear that "no experience is required." This is the image of the sales field, and it is unfortunately fostered by those who are supposed to be sales professionals.

There are others who realize that there is no magic, no easy way to the top. Sadly, they never apply for the job. Even though they may have great potential for success as salespeople, they are lost because the myths of sales drive them away.

Mostly, the problem centers around the persistent presentation of the so-called "sales personality," the glad-handling, gregarious, extroverted individual who glides smoothly into any situation, captures the attention of everyone he or she meets, and always comes away with the order. These are the people who can sell anything. And when you look at their resumes, there *is* a reason for this—they *have* sold just about anything that can be sold.

What's so damaging is the sinister implication that all you really need is a bag of clever closing techniques to make it really big in sales. And that's also why salespeople flock to expensive sales seminars. The same people go from one seminar to the next, hoping to pick up a trick or two that will automatically propel them to the top, that will transform them into super salespeople. Tell them that great salespeople are made, not born, and they'll sign up every time a huckster comes to town saying, "All you have to do is memorize the latest 43 sure-fire, knock 'em dead closing techniques and you're on your way to the big leagues. No one will be able to resist you. It's an order every time."

The myth of the "sales personality" is just that—a myth kept alive by those who need to be reassured constantly that they are really good...the best! What the sales field needs more than anything else is men and women who are committed to customers and who possess the competence necessary to represent their companies effectively. That's real sales, and there's nothing more honorable or rewarding.

Chapter
THIRTEEN

— ✧ —

Making Sales Happen

The Art of Closing a Deal

Graham's Law: The most objectionable of all
sales slogans is "Close on the objection."

UNDERSTANDING THE GAME RULES

When Ronald Reagan begot the idea for the Strategic Defense Initiative, an impenetrable shield that would zap an incoming nuclear missile with lasers, particles beams, and other Buck Rogers-style contraptions—critics scoffed. Today, the initiative is all but dead. But another defense shield is still in place, and even mightier. It's the one that most business people erect to protect themselves from the throngs of salespeople who would, if unchecked, soak up every minute of their day. Unfortunately, most salespeople don't realize what they're up against, so they go bouncing from one shield to another, until they find one with a crack.

By understanding what turns off potential customers, you'll get a much better idea of what not to do when trying to make a sale. Here are the primary ways that executives and others shield themselves from pesky salespeople:

1. *They avoid all salespersons who say, "I only need 20 minutes of your time."* No one in sales with any knowledge or experience would ever use such a stupid ploy. All the salesperson wants to do is try to unload something fast. Prospects can be sure there will be no effort to try to understand their needs or the problems they want to have solved.

2. *They dismiss the thought of meeting with the person who says, "I just want to stop by for a few minutes and get acquainted with you."* Smart business people know that this is the "friendly, nonthreatening approach," but when they reach out to shake hands, they'll encounter a cold fist. So they tell the person to take the necessary time and effort to get acquainted with their company before trying to squeeze a frantic foot in the door.

3. *They refuse to talk to anyone who calls on the phone and says, "Do you want to make some money?"* They know that if

173

they give such a caller the time of day, they'll get taken to the cleaners. (Actually, the best answer to such nonsense is simply to say, "No, I don't have time to make money. I'm so busy now that I won't be able to think about making money for at least another six months. Why don't you call me back then?")

4. *They don't waste their time reading letters that begin, "As an astute business leader, you know...."* As astute business leaders they've been around long enough not to be conned by a second-rate copywriter who believes that such transparent flattery pays big dividends. All they see is a warning to stop reading and to dismiss the message without giving it further thought.

5. *They never meet with anyone who says, "Hey, let's get together."* Behind that friendly facade is an agenda—and it's not theirs. They know their time will be wasted and they'll have to listen to a story that is (a) irrelevant to what they want to accomplish, (b) an attempt to sell them something they don't want to buy, and (c) an insult to their intelligence.

6. *They never talk to anyone who calls on the phone at 7:45 A.M. or 5:15 P.M.* They know these are always salespeople who just attended a one-day seminar on "How to succeed in sales without knowing what you're doing." Executives, they say, answer their own phones both before and after business hours. In fact, the salesperson may have them on the phone, but all this has done is guarantee that the prospect will never talk more than five seconds or give an appointment to see them.

7. *They abstain from reading anything that guarantees making them an expert in "60 seconds."* Seasoned business people know that if you're either dumb enough or desperate enough to believe that you can become anything other than ignorant in 60 seconds, then you deserve

what you'll get for your money—nothing. Those who publish such trash prey upon the "instant instincts" in each of us. Contrary to popular thought, quality and performance can only be achieved by intelligence and effort.

8. *They stay away from the salesperson who says, "All we need to do...."* They know that the quickest way to go into instant bankruptcy is falling for simple solutions. Let the guy with the "all we need to do" attitude start his own company and run it for awhile. That will wipe the smile off his face and make him suspicious of those who would have him buy such naive thinking. Whether we like it or not, there's still no magic.

9. *They don't let anyone sit down who says, "I'm impressed. You certainly have an interesting office."* Smart business people know that a salesperson who utters this phrase has just read a page out of the latest "How to make more sales" book. This is particularly true if the only decoration in your four- by six-foot office is a dead plant in the corner. Such shoddy techniques only reveal an ill-prepared product pusher who repeats the same line on every call.

10. *They don't go near anyone who says he wants to buy the business.* These people are not serious, of course. They only want to impress you. "I'd give anything to have a business like this," they intone. Veterans of the business world mentally reply, "Well, write out a check for $10 million and it's yours. If you don't have the money now, call me when you do. Thanks for stopping by." Salespeople who use phoney flattery don't even get the opportunity to tell their story.

Most of the "laser beams" in a prospect's shield will deactivate if the salesperson's company has been using the customer cultivation techniques described in the previous chapters. The few remaining ones will be withdrawn if the salesperson has been using what we call "the power of sales authority" to display a professional demeanor.

USING THE POWER OF
SALES AUTHORITY

If you're a salesperson reading this chapter, you may say that you would *never* make such obvious mistakes as those just mentioned. Yet, chances are, at least once you've called a prospect on the phone and said, "I assure you this will only take 20 minutes." Think about it for a moment. What right do you have to take 20 minutes of anyone's time? You may also forget that there are 10 other salespeople asking for "just 20 minutes" of a prospect's time every day of the week. That amounts to 900 hours a year!

Let's say that you do get the appointment. Chances are, you're going to first try to establish a rapport with the prospect (that's 10 minutes gone). Then you'll comment on the prospect's interesting desk or artwork. Then you'll glance at the prospect's bookcase and make a remark about one or two of the books. Finally, you'll try to close the sale, at which point you're shown the way to the door. This happens time and time again.

Now, here's the message: If you want to get through, then you should change your thinking—and your approach. Try thinking like a customer. Unfortunately, this is easier said than done. Though they try, most business-to-business salespeople have difficulty putting themselves in their customer's shoes. Maybe there's a barrier simply because they have never owned a business, held a management position, or been on "the buying side" of the desk. Yet, knowing the mental processes of a decision maker is essential to successful selling.

The highly successful, professional salesperson knows that to think like a buyer, you need to tap the hidden "power of sales authority," which consists of a series of elements that convey a strong, unified personal image. It doesn't make any difference whether you are 23 and still wet behind the ears or 59 and a sales veteran of 30 years—if you want to begin selling more, then put the power of authority to work. Here are the key elements:

1. *The way you look.* What about the quality of your clothes and shoes? The first thing a prospect sees when you go toward the chair is your shoes. Does your trench coat look as if it's been in the trenches for the past six months? What about your hair? Are your clothes clean and pressed? What about your watch and other jewelry? What do prospects think when they spot your plastic digital watch?

2. *The way you walk.* Are you confident and composed or do you give the impression that you're rushing around? Do you stand up straight or slouch? Remember, prospects want to deal with people who are in charge of themselves.

3. *The way you talk.* Are your words chosen carefully? What about your vocabulary? Your ability to express ideas precisely and accurately is the direct result of the words you have available. Is your voice deep and full? It should be if you want to inspire confidence.

4. *The way you make eye contact.* As much as any other factor, eye contact tells your story. Strong eye contact lets the prospect know that you are at ease yet in command of the situation, and that you feel comfortable with yourself, your products or services, and your ability to meet the prospect's needs.

5. *The way you open your briefcase.* When you go to open your briefcase, where are the prospect's eyes? Certainly, they are glued to what you're doing. Are your

materials organized or do you fumble around through a pile of papers? Is your briefcase leather or plastic? Leather makes its mark. At every point, the prospect is making a judgment about you. That's right. You!

6. *The way you take charge.* Do you just push everything around on the prospect's desk, as if nothing was more important to the prospect than to have his or her desk rearranged just for you? (Remember, this is the desk you were so impressed with just a few minutes ago!) Or, are you polite and considerate in asking for proper space to make your presentation? By the way, if you need more room, why not ask the prospect if you could move to a conference room? The prospect might even be impressed with your desire to make an effective presentation.

7. *The way you answer questions.* Are your answers direct and specific? Are you willing to be forthright in telling the prospect the limitations of your products or services, as well as the positive points? There's no perfect product. The prospect knows it and you know it. If prospects ask a question that stumps you, are you honest enough to say that you don't know the answer, but that you'll get it for them? That's a lot more impressive than trying to fake it. If you know you're faking it, so will the prospect! When you're honest, the prospect will have more confidence in you, your company, and what you're trying to sell.

8. *The way your materials look.* Are they professionally prepared? Or, do you pass out lousy photocopies? Are they organized or are they assembled as you go along? Do you scribble prices and comments in the margins? This just says that you're hauling around scrap paper.

Keep your materials pristine so the prospect can focus on the features and benefits.

The "authority close" begins the moment you walk through your customer's door. Every movement you make and every step you take is carefully calculated to lead your customer to one inevitable conclusion: To buy from you.

Most sales are lost not because the salesperson offers the wrong product, the wrong service, or the wrong price. *Sales are lost because the customer makes an unconscious mental decision to reject the person doing the selling.* Once this happens, the sale is gone, gone, gone. Nothing you do, including making price concessions, will get it back.

The goal in getting the order is to have prepared the way so well that there's no room for refusal. If a prospect can find a reason—any reason—to reject your offer, it becomes very easy for him or her to say "No." If the prospect can reject you, the salesperson, it is even easier! As frightening as it may seem, the decision to buy or not to buy is made in the first 60 seconds of your call. If you have created the right climate by understanding how the prospect thinks, then you have done the best you can in getting beyond the first minute. Now let's look at some techniques for actually closing deals.

SELLING TECHNIQUES THAT COMPLEMENT YOUR MAGNET MARKETING EFFORTS

For the sales pro, making the sale is success. It's the act of getting the order that towers above everything else. It's both very personal and powerful. This is what gets salespeople up in the morning and keeps them there all day.

In order to make the next call, the pro deliberately forgets about the slammed doors, the unreturned telephone calls, the lost sales. That's excess baggage. To carry it around would pull the pro down in the dumps. Yet, the lost sales cannot be forgotten. That's business never to be regained. That's business gone straight to someone else. The goal, then, is to increase the percentage of sales made—the time, effort, and money that goes into preparation, proposals, and meetings with prospects are all lost if the sale is lost.

Truly professional salespeople make it a point, above everything else, to learn the customer's agenda. They know that the major task of the salesperson is to get inside the head of the customer. How does the person think? What are the problems? What does the customer want to accomplish? That takes time to learn, to uncover. And it can't be discovered if your goal is simply to figure out the quickest and easiest way to get the customer to do what you want.

The pros also know that to make a sale, you have to learn how to make the customer's heart go pitter-patter. At first glance, this may sound more than a little silly. Some may even think it's total nonsense. It's not. Here's what we mean. We always look forward to visiting another person's business. Calling on a prospect gives us an opportunity to learn something new—and that's exciting. We've never found a business that's dull or boring. Yet, we see the eyes light up when the person across the desk senses our excitement. It is almost as if that individual is saying, "What am I missing in my own business that these guys seem to see?" In fact, that is exactly the issue. As an outsider, you see genuine excitement while the person who is involved in the business every day has become dulled by the ongoing routines.

The salesperson's job is to rekindle that enthusiasm—to make the prospect's adrenalin flow and spine tingle. More than anything else, people want to feel that they are involved in something interesting and exciting. The job of the salesperson is to make that happen.

Finally, successful salespeople learn to become priceless resources. Everybody talks about doing it, but the pressure to make the next sale places customer education on the back burner for most salespeople. Let's set the record straight: It isn't what you sell that's important. Rather, it's how the salesperson comes to be viewed by the customer that counts. The customer who thinks, "I want this guy around. He's got ideas I can use," will buy because that salesperson is valuable.

Follow these guidelines and your time will be more productive, your work will be more efficient, and you'll close more sales.

1. *Never use "boilerplate" proposals.* This should be so obvious it's not even necessary to mention it. Yet, it happens every day, even with the biggest firms. In other words, don't get lazy and fall victim to the power of the word processor. Customers aren't stupid. They can see through the *generic* proposal, one in which you just filled in the blanks. Unless they feel you took the necessary time and effort to prepare your proposal, they'll react negatively with more objections than you ever thought possible.

   Of course, it takes a lot more time to prepare a custom proposal for each customer or client. But that's what the customer expects—personal attention. If you can't give custom service when you're trying to make the sale, the customer will conclude that you won't give personal service after the sale. In other words, your proposal can be an important way to separate yourself from the competition.

2. *Whenever you make a promise, be sure you can keep it.* This idea can be phrased another way: Always tell the truth. Both inexperienced salespeople—as well as old pros—can fall into the trap of telling customers what they think they want to hear in order to keep them happy. Since "making the sale" is always like getting your name up in lights or climbing the highest moun-

tain, there's an incredible tendency to do anything and everything to get the order signed. Unfortunately, that also includes making promises that can—and often will—come back to haunt you, particularly when it's time to go to that customer to make the next sale.

3. *Always sell what the customer needs.* This is perhaps the most difficult issue of all because it cuts two ways. On the one hand, your expertise indicates a specific recommendation. But the customer doesn't want to spend that much. As a result, the sale goes through for something that you know will not be of benefit.

   Then, there's the situation when you know that the middle priced model or service would meet the customer's requirements, but selling all the bells and whistles would be easy. In both cases, the rule is: Never let any sale go through without making your appraisal of the situation totally clear to the customer. When the customer discovers what has happened, you want to keep your relationship strong. If your customer feels *taken,* it will be your last sale.

4. *If a customer has a problem, be ready to accept personal responsibility.* If your ego won't allow you to do this, then you shouldn't be in sales. Never blame a difficulty on anyone else or another department in your company. This is a common problem among salespeople. They want to "keep their skirts clean." As a result, they're quick to make it clear that they are not the ones who made the mistake. A company's credibility is always at stake. If your customer begins to feel that your firm does not present a unified front, then you are eroding your base of confidence. This will result in lost sales, either now or in the future.

5. *Maintain close contact after the sale.* Since good salespeople are always looking for the next mountain to climb, they tend to forget that the word *customer* implies a continuing relationship with the salesperson and not the service department or a junior accountant in the case of a CPA firm. The customer bought *you*, the salesperson. *You* are the one who cultivated the sales. *You* are the one who said "thank you" for the order. *You* are the one who answered the questions and negotiated the deal. If you ignore the customer after the sale, it's like being jilted, which is something the customer will never forget. You will have made your first—and last—sale.

6. *Make your customers feel important.* There's nothing worse than a salesperson making a customer feel insignificant. Yet, it happens every day. In an effort to make a strong impression, someone will say, "Just last week, Gotcha Corp., the international conglomerate, bought 1000 of our computers." That's great, but how does it make someone feel who is buying one, two, or three? Pretty small. Congratulate customers for *their* achievements. Comment on positive things about a business. Life in the trenches isn't always easy, so making people feel good about what they are doing gives a boost that will not be forgotten.

7. *Make sure the customer sees you as your company's representative.* There's a subtle tendency among some of the best salespeople to want to separate themselves from the company they represent. This comes from wanting to feel that they are the ones who made the sale. It's their ability, their expertise, and their skill that got the job done. It's as if they are doing their company a favor to be out there doing such a great job.

   These are the people whose commitment is 100 percent—to themselves and not to the company. They always keep an emotional door open so they can quickly move on to the next position without any regrets. Just remember that customers are experienced, too. They can tell the differences in salespeople. They know the difference between *pros* who are really in business for themselves and those who are dedicated to the best interests of the companies they represent.

8. *Even though it's easy to push for the sale, be willing to wait.* What distinguishes the outstanding salesperson from all the others is one significant quality: The real pro knows when to be patient and willing to wait for the sale. We all like the customer who buys quickly, the one who responds fast. But that's only one type of customer. There are many others who are more cautious and ponder the possibilities before they close a deal.

   In many ways, your best customers of all are in this latter group. They're committed. Once they have made a decision, they stay with you over the long haul. In fact, most sales are lost because the salesperson pushes too hard and tries to hustle the customer. At least that's the way it comes across. The customer resists what appears to be "pressure," and gets turned off. It's then that the sale is lost—to someone else who is willing to be patient.

In today's highly competitive business environment, selling is a tough profession. That's what makes it so exciting and rewarding. The "order takers" fall fast when the competition is keen. Only the professional salesperson survives and prospers when the going gets tough. Just about anyone will be able to sell a $500 fax machine until the market is saturated. Neither skill nor talent is required to move products when prices are falling. It takes a pro to sell a $4,000 fax machine today!

If you want to be the best in sales, then you'll have to take the professional approach. In the long run, you'll have more customers, more sales, and a lot more respect.

SUMMARY

The devotees of traditional sales methods will view the customer development concept as slow, cumbersome, and not sufficiently aggressive. They want more push and drive. More power. Bigger and better results. Of course, it is possible to "crash through" sales now and then and achieve stunning results. But you cannot plan for the long-term and growth without consistently strong sales. And for salespeople to be able to consistently close deals, your company must use marketing to provide solid, qualified leads on a regular basis. This makes it possible for salespeople to actually sell and not just spin their wheels.

Which brings us full circle to Chapter 1 of this book—how marketing and salespeople must work together in concert. In earlier chapters, we've given you the basics you need to launch a magnet marketing program in your company. Perhaps you're already off and running with new ideas. But equally likely, you might be wondering how to sell the magnet marketing concept to your colleagues and superiors. Chapter 14 will give you some insights into the internal sales process.

———— ✧ ————

Creating a Department of Customer Cultivation

The Art of Managing Marketing Information

Graham's Law: Customers don't grow on trees—you have to nurture them for days with tender loving care and lots of patience.

THE CURE FOR INFORMATION ANXIETY

We know of a furniture company that spent $20,000 on a market research study. The two-inch-thick report was the topic of a half-hour "strategic meeting." A day later, all 18 copies of the "top secret" report made their way down to the company's storage bin in the basement.

The sales department of another company, a large electrical supply company we know, spent $150,000 on a state-of-the-art computer system that could be used to maintain comprehensive customer records. Yes, the company now has state-of-the-art records, but no one in the company knows what to do with them. So the computer system has become the world's most expensive mailing label generator.

Then there's the customer service department of a large department store chain that completed a study about its most prevalent complaints. The report was circulated to all customer service reps, who agreed with the findings. But they were too busy keeping up with business as usual to translate the report into an action plan that would help reduce future complaints.

Today, largely because of the computer, we are awash in a sea of information. Some customer, market, and competitive information is invaluable, but never makes it to the right eyes. Conversely, some information is useless, but clogs the desks and mailboxes of business people throughout the nation. In any case, the time, money, and energy that goes into gathering information is rarely translated into actions that achieve the company's goal of creating customers.

Fortunately, companies can put their information to good use by creating what we call the "Department of Customer Cultivation." The Department serves as a conduit through which marketing people can receive vital information about customers, the marketplace, and the competitive arena. It also serves as an information pipeline that links everyone in the company, including people who are normally "behind-the-scenes" (designers, engineers, and manufacturing managers) or "after-the-fact" (customer service reps).

Why is the flow of information so vital? Because even though the cultivation process is largely carried out by marketing people, the marketing department alone cannot create customers. The cultivation of customers entails sharing information from all parts of the company, information that can lead to effective techniques, strategies, and plans for attracting and keeping customers. In fact, it is only through the combined effort of everyone in the company that the cultivation process becomes possible.

Consider a manufacturing company. If designers, engineers, and production people had an opportunity to exchange information with the people who actually promote and sell products, they'd be able to make goods that customers really want and need. This, in turn, would arm the marketing people with a competitive tool: a product line that truly makes the company the vendor of choice.

Likewise, if customer service people are included in the cultivation process, they can report the kinds of problems that incense customers and cause the company to lose repeat business. The production department can then correct the problems and give marketing people the kind of products that will bring customers to the company on their own accord.

As an illustration of the crying need for Departments of Customer Cultivation, think about laptop computer makers. Every industry pundit who reviews laptop computers laments the fact that most manufacturers have gotten some aspect of the computer "right," while falling short on others:

"Great screen, lousy keyboard"
"Great keyboard, lousy screen"
"Great screen, great keyboard, but it's too big and heavy"
"Nice and small, but the batteries don't last long enough."
And so on.

The first manufacturer to achieve the optimal blend of functionality, readability, and portability will find an army of customers beating a path to his door, and that will only happen when everyone involved with the product pools their knowledge of the marketplace.

The same principles apply to service or professional services companies, where the cultivation of customers depends on the flow and feedback of information. No real estate, insurance, or engineering firm can succeed by having its marketing, salespeople, brokers, or professional people operate in a vacuum. Only a wholistic effort, in which the cultivation process is greater than the sum of the parts, will allow the firm to succeed in good times and bad times alike.

UP THE NEW ORGANIZATIONAL CHART

Just where does this Department of Customer Cultivation fit into the organizational chart? Is it appended to the marketing division? To the Sales Department? To top management? None of the above—it cuts across *all* divisions and exists as a "virtual" department—that is, it exists as a concept, not an actual entity. In fact, you can build a Department of Customer Cultivation without breaking down administratively separate divisions. All you need to do to launch the department is to get representatives from key divisions to share their insights and work towards the common goal of attracting new customers and keeping old ones.

Marketing people should probably manage the Department of Customer Cultivation, since they're the ones who will devise tactics for creating a positive buying environment. *Manage* in this sense means sponsoring regular feedback forums and proposing concrete plans of action based on the shared information. The forums can be formal or informal and held as often as your company needs to build a strong cultivation plan.

Ideally, top management should attend the forums because their presence signals a vote of confidence and validates the cultivation process. Moreover, the outcome of the forums directly affects top management's ability to achieve its goals. So it behooves top managers to get a firsthand glimpse of how various departments plan to spend their time and money. (By the way, idea sharing forums can work in a company of 10 or 10,000. Giant textile maker Milliken sponsors a "sharing rally" each month, in which 50 representatives from various divisions swap ideas about improving operations, customer service, and so on. In the last eight years, the chairman and president of the company have never missed a rally. Now that's top management support!)

THE DEPARTMENT OF CUSTOMER CULTIVATION IN ACTION

Beyond sponsoring feedback forums, marketing people must establish a set of cultivation objectives for the new department, such as how they want customers to perceive them, what areas of expertise they can pass along to customers, and so on.

Once a company has established and quantified its cultivation objectives, it can develop strategic programs based on market research and knowledge of competitive activity. These strategies must then be converted to tactical activities.

Despite the opportunities for greater market share and long-term success that can be achieved through customer cultivation, you might find that the concept meets with some degree of skepticism at first. The most serious one relates to selling a concept that, at first blush, appears to be arrogant: "If you want to do business with us, then you must come to us."

Many people might consider the concept too passive and therefore too risky. You can counter the argument by explaining how firms that successfully cultivate customers do so very aggressively. Once you've gotten beyond the major conceptual hurdle, you can anticipate the following kinds of objections:

1. *Our salespeople cultivate our customers.* On the surface, this seems to make sense, but as we've stressed throughout this book, it expresses a total misunderstanding of the separate roles of sales and marketing. Explain to top management that the role of marketing is not to make sales—it is to create the right conditions so that more sales can be made. In some cases, it is to give support so that a sales force is more effective. Other times, it is to provide leads. But at all times, it is to create a pre-existing climate so that prospective customers want to do business with you.

2. *We already know where our customers are.* The implication of this line of thinking is that the company has totally identified its market. This is usually an illusion; you can't know where your customers are without an ongoing cultivation process. One of the chief roles of an effective marketing program is the continual cultivation of existing customers, as well as the uncovering of prospects. In today's competitive environment, that process should be constant and intense. Besides, even if you do know where your customers are, some thought should be given to the unavoidable fact that your competition knows where they are, too.

3. *The only thing important to our customers is price.* This always sounds so hard-hitting and utterly businesslike, but it has no basis. One recent study of business-to-business purchasing found that only six percent of all purchases are based strictly on price. Anyone trying to build or sustain a business on price alone won't be around long. One of the essential goals of the cultivation process is to create a climate in which people will want to do business with you. When that happens, price alone becomes a minor concern.

4. *We rely on word of mouth for new business.* Of course, any strong business relies on word-of-mouth advertising, but the word-of-mouth process can be made substantially more effective. One of the outcomes of the cultivation process should be to enhance the customers' understanding of why they should do business with your company; in other words, to give people a new rationale for why they became customers in the first place. That is accomplished through magnet marketing techniques of self-promotion, media relations, and advertising.

5. *We don't need to cultivate customers because everybody knows us.* Tell that one to McDonald's because they'll be glad to save all their marketing money. Firstly, everybody does not know your company, whether you are large or small. Secondly, everybody does not think of you when considering a buying decision. If that were the case, only one insurance agency would survive in a community—or one of any other business for that matter. Every company must cultivate customers every hour of the day if it intends to stay in business over the long term.

6. *Our sales are great, so why waste money cultivating customers?* Is it really good business to carry on a marketing program when sales are strong? The smartest companies market the heaviest during "the best times of the year." Why would anyone want to do that? Because the marketing process has a cumulative effect—and many times a delayed reaction. Just because you're out there marketing your products or services doesn't mean that a particular customer is ready for you. Yet, when the need arises, they'll call! That's what customer cultivation is all about.

7. *Customer cultivation is only for big companies.* Even among very successful business people, there is the mistaken notion that smaller companies cannot really get into marketing. The scale of the effort may be different, but any size company can, and should, have a customer cultivation program, including specific short- and long-term goals and objectives.

Unfortunately, in smaller companies, so-called "marketing money" is often wasted on irrelevant and meaningless items such as four-color brochures. Smaller companies need the best customer cultivation guidance and advice they can get in order to avoid wasting money and to compete effectively. No matter who we are or what business we're in, we must cultivate customers. It just so happens that some do it better—and smarter— than others.

Every company must think in terms of cultivating customers if it is to compete effectively, grow, and prosper, and it doesn't matter whether you accept the idea of a Department of Customer Cultivation or not. All that matters is your willingness to commit the time and resources necessary to make your cultivation efforts pay off through a unified, company-wide effort that brings to bear the company's total resources on the shared goal of attracting and holding customers; that is, of conducting effective magnet marketing.

———— ✧ ————

Chapter FIFTEEN

Igniting the Engines of Change

How to Institute a New Marketing and Sales Program

*Graham's Law: If your company keeps doing
it the old way, you'll double your
competition's sales.*

ACTIONS SPEAK LOUDER THAN WORDS

Question: When is the best time to embark on a new approach to marketing and sales? Answer: Now. If your company is a one-man band, making a change is easy. But what about a large organization with a sales department, a marketing department, and a suite of top managers? Making change is not always so simple. Regardless of your position, it's important to understand the kind of barriers you might encounter and to develop appropriate strategies for overcoming them. Here are some basic impediments to change.

THE TOUGH HIDE SYNDROME

Question: What is the primary motivation for making change in a business?

A. Greater profits

B. Greater efficiency

C. Better competitive posture

D. Fear

E. None of the above

Most business people won't admit it, but they're primarily driven by choice "D" Fear. Nothing drives a company to action like the fear of the bill collector or the tax collector. This attitude is quite prevalent in the domestic manufacturing world, where very few companies have taken advantage of state-of-the-art techniques for improving quality, customer service, and overall profitability. Only the threat of lower priced goods from Japan and other Pacific Rim nations has forced American companies to consider changing their production methods.

Nonmanufacturing companies also operate on the fear principle. A giant retailer might not feel compelled to take action until a competitor has surrounded him with bargain basement outlets. A bank might suddenly feel the pinch when the only lines at the teller windows are those of the institution across the street. And a consultant might only reach for the rolodex and telephone when he suddenly realizes that his checkbook will be empty in six weeks.

Why do business people wait until the hammer falls? In part, it's a matter of human nature. Most people find it easier to limp along with a mild toothache than to muster up the courage to see the dentist. Only when the tooth becomes intolerably painful do we think about picking up the telephone and getting help.

The reason for our procrastination has to do with "magical thinking." Though we like to think of ourselves as rational and analytical human beings, in the face of adversity many of us voyage to a childlike magical world in which problems vanish when we put them out of our minds. A related action is to acknowledge that a problem exists, but to fight it with a war of attrition. The thinking goes like this: Let it go long enough, and it will just disappear.

Of course, many business problems do vanish by themselves. But in retrospect, we usually find that they weren't really problems at all—just minor aberrations within our companies or the marketplace. Real problems in finance, marketing, sales, manufacturing, purchasing, and distribution don't go away. At times they cause less pain, but if untreated they may prove to be seriously destructive, even fatal.

When it comes to initiating marketing programs, no company can afford to wait until competitors are racing by at warp speed or sales have dwindled to an alarmingly low level. If people in your company deny that anything is wrong, do whatever you can to scare them into taking action. Conduct psychological warfare to make them feel that the pain has suddenly escalated and that immediate action is necessary for the survival of the company. Once you've pierced the tough hides surrounding their brains, you may be able to launch new customer cultivation initiatives that create the kind of buying environment you need to attract and retain customers.

THE INERTIA SYNDROME

Remember Sisyphus? He was the guy in the Greek myth who was condemned by the gods to roll a giant ball up a mountain, only to see it career back down to the bottom each time he neared the top. Poor Sisyphus just couldn't get past the final hump to achieve victory.

Like Sisyphus, all of us face a final hump that we must overcome to get a project rolling. We all experience inertia problems in our personal and business lives. It takes a tremendous amount of energy to start dieting, start exercising, or begin a major clean out of the attic. It takes even more energy to introduce changes in the way a company does marketing and sales. And it takes a tremendous jolt to introduce seemingly radical marketing concepts.

What causes the inertia? To be human is to tune out whatever upsets our equilibrium. This "cognitive dissonance," as psychologists call it, affects business, as well as every other type of human pursuit. Look back at history and you'll see countless examples of people who were burned at the stake because they upset everyday equilibrium by challenging the conventional wisdom of the known world.

Even in more modern times, people who have caused ripples have paid a price. Galileo was placed under the equivalent of "house arrest" for his astronomical theories. Newton was initially ridiculed for his thoughts on gravity, and Einstein was considered crazy for challenging the Newtonian viewpoint. Eventually, seemingly "outlandish" ideas can and do become the norm and remain so until the next "outlandish" thought disrupts the *status quo*.

Businesspeople, especially those in marketing and sales, are equally gun shy about new ideas. They would rather accept the limitations of their present way of doing business than accept the risk of adopting a new framework. Unless they start thinking differently, no progress is possible, especially when it comes to marketing and sales.

THE LAURELS SYNDROME

"Things started off great," said the owner of a small consulting firm. "The first four years kept getting better and better." That was eight years ago. Today, this same owner isn't sure he can keep the doors open much longer. Today his personal income has dropped below what it was when he began the business. "I didn't think too much about it when income leveled off for a couple of years," he adds. "Business was still good so I thought it was just a change in the industry." The *change* kept right on going—downhill. Now, his business is in a steep decline and he isn't sure what happened.

Another business owner tells the same story. When he bought the 50-year-old service company, it had a good track record. With the new ownership, sales began to increase. The business expanded. "I had over 30 employees a couple of years ago. Now I have three."

These business experiences illustrate what we call the Rise and Fall Cycle and it forms an almost perfect bell curve. The start-up period is one of sharp growth, which is followed by a time of slowing down and leveling off. Then comes the downhill slide. This pattern is more than just interesting. It is the history of a growing number of businesses large and small and the dynamics in every case are almost identical. Here's what happens:

The businesses are started by skilled, talented, and motivated individuals who see a particular niche for their

products or services. The founders have years of experience working for firms in a particular industry. So they
start a business that capitalizes on the relationships
they have built up over the past 20 or more years. The
door of opportunity is wide open and they are daring
enough to take advantage of it.

From the moment they go into business, they have a
lot of confidence and they do well. Drawing upon their
contacts, business comes their way. Some even make arrangements to take over the work they were doing for a
former employer. In fact, this is a familiar scenario
among these businesses and the "big boost" that gets
them going fast.

The owner's contacts have an immediate payoff. Because these entrepreneurs are well known in their industry, they are able to attract business quickly. A
snowball effect begins. By keeping in touch with the
people they know, more and more business flows to
them quickly and easily. It appears this process takes
between three and five years to reach its peak.

Next, a leveling off period sets in. This seems to last
for two or three years. Sales don't drop but they don't
go up, either. Nevertheless, something very, very important is taking place, and it is only with hindsight that
the picture becomes clear to the business owner.

What's happening during this no-growth period?
Why does the business lose its original momentum?
The customers who gave the original impetus to the operation begin to disappear. The owner's key contact in a
firm takes another position and the new person has his
or her own suppliers. At first, this only means a loss of a
percentage of the business, but, as time goes on, accounts get smaller and then begin to disappear.

At the same time, some of the original clients begin
to disappear as they retire, change jobs, get fired, and so

on. In other words, an erosion process takes place. Some accounts are replaced by new ones, but the momentum has diminished and the company is simply "holding its own."

Finally, the decline begins and then accelerates. Many of those customers who gave the business its start-up power have disappeared completely. New customers are not as prestigious as the ones who gave the enterprise its initial impetus because the business owner now lacks the "influence" that he had with friends and associates in the early days.

At this point, it is common for the business owner to say that he is working harder now than when he first went into business. There is an intense effort during the decline to get new business, but it is more and more difficult to attract quality customers.

When you look closely at these businesses, there are some fascinating similarities. First, despite their problems, the owners are quite competent in their fields. Second, the owners are, for the most part, good business people and they have the necessary experience and confidence to operate their own companies. They didn't just run out and start a business without possessing the knowledge required to operate a company. Third, the owners are capable managers. They attract and keep quality employees. In fact, there appears to be considerable loyalty among those who work for these firms. Finally, these are not people who abused their businesses. With one exception, we have found these owners deeply committed to their enterprises. There is no indication that they have drained their businesses of necessary capital.

At the same time, our analysis indicates other trends among these business owners.

1. *They are victims of their initial success.* Because the businesses grew quickly—sometimes almost effortlessly—the owners concluded that they had "a magic touch." Because, in some cases, they succeeded beyond their wildest dreams, they really thought that they had what it takes to be successful. They did not recognize that their success was the direct result of the contacts they had built up over the previous decade or so.

2. *These business owners assumed that their success would continue—automatically.* It's easy to be critical of such an assumption. Even the owners realize their naivete in hindsight. But, at the time a business is experiencing new sales records every month, it is natural to conclude that the roll will continue.

3. *During the leveling off period, owners give logical explanations for the changes in their businesses.* "At first, I said it was the economy," comments one man. "Then, I attributed the problem to some of the changes we had in our own personnel." Such explanations for no-growth are indeed logical. They make sense to the owners. As a result, they seem to avoid any deeper analysis of their problems. It's almost as if they're afraid to look too closely at the situation because of what they might find.

4. *It is only when the decline is well underway that more serious questions are asked.* Those going into business tend to be optimistic. They believe that more effort is all that's needed to solve problems. And, most important of all, they think things will change for the better tomorrow. It is only when sales continue to drop lower and lower that the owner says he needs help.

If these businesses were generally well managed, offered quality products and services, and had adequate capital, at least during the growth period, why did they find themselves in such deep, deep trouble? In every case—without exception—we discovered they never had an effective marketing program. Most of them did not have anything that even resembled a well-defined marketing program. Although the owners gave lip service to marketing, there were no budgets to prove their commitment.

"It didn't seem important," one quite candid owner said. "Things were going so well, there was no need to try to get more business. I would have considered marketing a waste of money. If you had talked to me in those days, I wouldn't have given you 10 minutes of my time."

Over and over again, the same story is repeated. "Since business was coming through the door, why should I have spent time and money on advertising and public relations?" another commented. It was only when the decline in sales was actually threatening the life of the business that these owners began thinking about marketing. In some cases, the cure was too late—and too costly. The resources were thin. As a result, limping along as best they could was the solution for some.

Would marketing have helped them survive? If, from the beginning, these same owners could have understood the cycle their businesses would go through over the first 10 years, they may have acted differently.

If they had understood from day one that the time was coming when their start-up customers would begin to disappear, they may have taken a different course. They may have seen the value of implementing a strong, unified, continual marketing effort aimed at both attracting new customers and keeping the ones already on the books.

Some did not even learn from their competitors. "We do a much better job for our clients than my major competitor. This is what our clients tell us. But my competitor never stops promoting his company throughout the industry." Unfortunately, that insight came only in hindsight.

What this scenario suggests is that marketing during periods of growth is absolutely essential to the long-term success of a business enterprise. It is when a company is on the move that it must assure its future stability and strength by doing everything possible to solidify its market position. This is what avoids trouble.

Even when the period of decline is underway, it is not too late to initiate a marketing program. Difficult situations can be turned around. But in order for that to happen, there must be a commitment to budget sufficient funds to achieve the required results.

Simple bandages can't cover deep wounds. Some companies recognize the value of borrowing money to upgrade their facilities or equipment in order to be more competitive. Those firms that want to change the direction of their sales curves must be willing to make the same investment in marketing. Conversely, when marketing is either ignored or viewed as an option that can be delayed until later, the seeds of decline are being sown and the Laurel's Syndrome will soon claim another victim.

THE CURE

Any of the above syndromes can be an impediment to bringing about much needed change in your company. To rid your company of them, you must become a torch bearer and spread the concept of customer cultivation. For the idea to take hold, though, it must function like a virus, reproducing itself in the minds of other people. This can only be done by pushing your idea relentlessly.

Firstly, develop a magnet marketing plan that shows how you can afford to budget for the main magnet marketing techniques described in Chapters 5, 6 and 7. Give some hypothetical results of the effects of a concerted self-promotional, media relations, and advertising campaign. Such a plan will strike fear into the hearts of everyone in your organization! Hopefully, it will shake them free from their everyday realities and enable them to consider alternatives. (Don't worry about rejection—you'll experience plenty of it. This is the only way incompetents are able to deal with good, solid thinking.)

As you present your plan(s), always smile. No matter what happens—smile. Your goal is to disarm the enemy. People will wonder what you're up to next. Since the business environment tends to foster paranoia, you will be viewed as someone with the inside track. As a result, you will be both loved and hated. There's one occasion when your broadest smile is essential: It occurs when someone shoots your ideas full of holes. If you smile correctly, the person working you over will think that it was all a setup. As a result, you're home free when you resubmit your plan.

After you get people to begrudge the fact that your plan might work, grab whatever money is offered—you can't make your program without a marketing budget. There's always a tendency to short change the marketing department, particularly when you come up with innovative ideas. Watch out for those who praise your creativity and then make sure you can't get the budget to implement your program. There is, however, an easy way to get the money you need to be effective. Don't ask for monumental sums. Get the pieces approved one by one. In other words, build your budget over a period of time, project by project. Such creativity is worthy of the highest marketing award.

Finally, when you do get commitment, be sure to stage a "signing ceremony." Your major task is to get a commitment from management that yours will be a company fueled by customer cultivation and other magnet marketing techniques. But don't be deceived. You'll hear words, words, and more words. Most of them will praise marketing and you'll think the top brass are on your team. Ignore all their words. Get it in writing. Prepare a magnet marketing statement and ask management to sign it. Make a thousand copies—you'll need them several times a day!

Of course, this is tongue and cheek. But it's no joke that you've got to work at making your point stick. Develop a realistic plan, back it up with numbers, propose a pilot, and get as much high-level support as you can. If you can do all these and make magnet marketing your personal crusade, you'll probably succeed. If not, you just might be playing on the wrong team.

Chapter
SIXTEEN

———— ✧ ————

Marketing in the 1990s

How to Get to the Year 2000 and Still Be in Business

Graham's Law: The future belongs to those who create it.

PRE-MILLENNIUM THINKING

The excitement's building. A new century—and a new millennium—are on the horizon. The decade of the 1980s came and went faster than any decade of recent memory. Now we're poised for the final step into the 21st century. What will the next 10 years hold for business? What effect will 1992 bring to the table when the entire continent of Europe becomes a single marketplace? What hand will new technology deal businesses? And, will we make it through the last days of the old century without serious economic upheaval?

Survival during the next decade may not be as simple as most of us may hope it will be. Insurance agencies, which have been disappearing by the thousands in recent years, will have their ranks thinned by still another third. The number of automobile dealerships will be cut in half. The small ones will go first, just as they have in the last 15 years.

In retail, the malls appear to be getting bigger and bigger as consumers seem to respond to the idea of "the shopping experience." Specifically, "shopping as entertainment" will more and more take the stage as the way to move merchandise. The small independent retailer will feel the squeeze. The story will not be much different for most businesses.

The present decade holds an important lesson for everyone in business; namely: Security is an illusion. If you don't believe it, just ask anyone at Wang or GM or a host of other "nothing can change things here" companies. All bets are off when it comes to who's going to make it.

All this suggests that "thrival and survival" in the years ahead depend, to a large degree, on the ability of a company to market itself effectively. There is already a new recognition of the necessity of marketing. More and more we hear business people saying, "You know, we've never had to market, but the time has come for us to take the initiative."

We think three basic marketing actions can give companies the power to grow and prosper in the year 2000:

The first is customer education. Since the mid–1980s, businesses have taken up the "service crusade" in an attempt to both gain and retain customers. Almost overnight, the consultants appeared at the door, while dozens of brochures proclaimed the possibility of attaining service perfection through one-day seminars. Books have oozed off the presses and even an international quality service association began carrying the banner across the world.

Better and better service was the business fetish of the 1980s. But to get through the coming decade successfully, customer education will be the primary issue. The change of focus will be profound, not cosmetic. Those firms that invest the effort and energy in providing their customers with helpful information and with expertise will be the winners.

For example, the CPA firms that continue to offer little more than number crunching will fade, while those providing business consulting services will prosper. In every area, the task will be to take a company's accumulated knowledge and make it available to the customer.

In fact, the best marketing will center around the education issue. Taking the time to organize and communicate information that will benefit customers will set the survivors apart from all other businesses. In these companies, the consultant role will supersede that of the salesperson.

It should be clear, however, that the problem is not one of simply doing a better job communicating the benefits of a firm's products or services. That's propaganda, not education. Rather, sales will flow from an approach that concentrates on recognizing the problems and needs of businesses and then providing the help required to solve them.

The second marketing action of the 1990s is what we call "company identification." Here the goal is to achieve the highest possible degree of uniqueness in the marketplace. It is to work to gain instant recognition and acceptance. When customers or prospects think of you, they must have a clear, undistorted, and accurate picture of who you are, what you do, and why you are different from other similar companies.

This is not a matter of posturing or slapping on a coat of paint to make the business look better. The issue runs deep and extends from the quality of a company's personnel to the image it portrays in the marketplace. But more than anything else, it involves taking the major assets of a firm—its people, products, and services—and developing a coordinated, cohesive, and unified program to communicate the message. This is what sets one company apart from another. Effort in this area will pay enormous dividends, particularly as competition heats up from new, highly energetic companies that are out to conquer your customers.

The third action is niche cultivation. This idea has been around for years. But the coming decade will require that niche development or niche marketing take a new direction for businesses. The difference is simple: Instead of carving out your particular niche, the task will be constantly seeking new niches while simultaneously cultivating a series of market segments. As you bounce three balls at the same time, you will also be adding new ones and letting others rest for a while.

Multi-niche development is complicated and demanding, requiring vision, risk, and constant vigil—qualities that, more often than not, are absent from current business thinking. Nevertheless, this is the stuff out of which success is built.

Together, customer education, company identification, and niche cultivation comprise the marketing mix for the 1990s. They represent the engine that will power a company across whatever problems and pitfalls it may encounter in the years ahead. Even more important, it is this mix that will enable a company to control its own destiny.

———— ◇ ————

Magnet Marketing Tactics—Roundup

The following tactics have all been discussed earlier in this book in the context of magnet marketing strategies. Keep this list handy when you're wondering what else you could be doing to attract and hold customers:

1. *Do some research.* Find out where your customers are coming from, their image of your business, and why they are doing business with you. Use this information to position your products or services.

2. *Publish your own newsletter.* Write articles that will be of interest to your audience. Include photos and graphics to grab your readers. A newsletter keeps you in front of your customers and prospects on a regular basis.

3. *Plan events to mark special occasions.* Hold an open house. Plan an anniversary celebration (promote your company's growth and stability). Make a ground-breaking exciting. Create a fun occasion—"The 153rd Anniversary of Weekly Steamboat Service between Buffalo and Fort Dearborn."

4. *Develop a mailing list.* Think of your mailing list as "the pot of gold at the end of the rainbow." Include prospects, present customers, and past customers. Build a special "druthers list"—those companies with which you would like to do business.

5. *Participate in trade shows.* Design an attractive booth exhibit and make sure your employees are trained to present your story effectively. Have a follow-up plan ready for "after-the-show" action.

6. *Issue news releases.* Keep the media informed about developments in your company—new products and services, employee promotions, awards presented to your firm, special events, seminars, and so on. Be sure to include a contact name and telephone number in your releases.

7. *Develop a customer-oriented brochure.* An effective brochure is one that gets your message across using a customer-oriented approach. Focus on how you solve problems and meet needs. Forget about how big and wonderful you think you are!

8. *Reprint news stories about your company.* Send reprints of articles about your company to customers, employees, and prospects. Everyone wants to be associated with a company receiving positive media exposure.

9. *Use direct mail.* Whether you use personalized letters (no "Dear Customer" letters, please) or self-mailers, get the word out *regularly* as a reminder of what you can do for customers and prospects. Direct mail is still the most cost-effective way to target your audience.

10. *Develop a consistent advertising program.* When you have positioned your company, stick with the image you have created and have all your advertising reflect your message. If you present conflicting images to your public, readers, viewers and listeners will be confused. Don't just think of the print media; radio and TV (including cable) may be useful to your campaign.

11. *Include response cards in your mailings.* You can use response cards to ask for immediate action. The cards are an excellent way for customers and prospects to ask for additional information, indicate a change of address, request a meeting, or place an order.

12. *Write articles for business publications.* You are an expert in your field. Your knowledge and experience can be the basis for helpful, informative articles in business publications.

13. *Use advertising specialties to promote your business.* No form of advertising has a higher exposure rating than

calendars, coffee mugs, executive gifts, and other carefully selected advertising specialties. A 400-sheet "note pad cube" has a life expectancy of more than six months. Showing your appreciation helps retain and attract customers.

14. *Sponsor seminars.* Invite your clients and prospects to seminars on timely topics. Make sure these sessions focus on issues of interest to those you are inviting. Be sure to invite the media and issue your own press releases.

15. *Produce a slide show or videotape.* Use a visual production to enhance your presentations, training programs, trade show exhibit, and so on. Your story will come to life. Quality counts, so avoid "homemade" productions.

16. *Conduct surveys.* Find out what customers and prospects are thinking. Surveys demonstrate that you're interested and concerned. Send out an opinion survey on a popular topic related to your business. Then, report the results to the media, as well as those who participated in the survey.

17. *Distribute helpful information.* Mail copies of interesting articles, studies and reports to customers and prospects. Your thoughtfulness will be appreciated and you will be recognized as a knowledgeable source.

18. *Seek speaking engagements.* Establish credibility, as well as visibility, with preferred audiences. You will soon be recognized as "the expert." Again, remember to invite the media to cover the occasion.

19. *Sponsor a community relations program.* Your company's involvement in "building a better community" sets you apart from your competitors and provides a basis for special recognition and media coverage.

20. *Dress for success.* Every impression should be a good one, including the way you dress. It's more important than you might think!

21. *Stay on track.* Good intentions don't increase sales. Once you develop a program make sure it is implemented on a continuing basis. That takes commitment. The results will be rewarding—getting and keeping customers.

--------- ✧ ---------

Graham'sLaws
Revisted

- If you think you know everything about selling, why aren't you selling everything?

- If you have a "Sales and Marketing" department, you are undoubtedly doing a lot of other things backwards, too.

- Attending sales seminars will always boost sales—for the speaker.

- Techniques don't make sales.

- If you're not growing prospects today, you won't have any customers tomorrow.

- If you don't tell your story, why should you expect anyone to know what you sell?

- If you think the media is the enemy, you don't know a friend when you see one.

- Anyone who says, "Advertising doesn't work," has been running a lousy ad campaign.

- If you're not educating, you're not selling.

- If you're not cultivating present customers, you're not growing your company.

- You may not be a box of soap, but your packaging is still important.

- There's only one valid assumption in business: The road ahead is always uphill.

- Absolutely nothing sells itself.

- The most objectionable of all sales slogans is "Close on the objection."

- Customers don't grow on trees—you have to nurture them for days with tender loving care and lots of patience.

- If your company keeps doing it the old way, you'll double your competition's sales.

- The future belongs to those who create it.

⬧

Ten Commandments for Losing Customers

Losing customers requires just as much effort as winning them. You must work at it as hard as the person who wants to be number one. Are you a winner—or a loser? Just like winners, losers develop a pattern of "success." Here are the guidelines: The Ten Commandments for Losing Sales:

1. ALWAYS HAVE AN EXCUSE   Develop a series of phrases and rehearse them regularly so you'll always have one ready when needed. Examples: "My car wouldn't start," "Our prices are too high," "The alarm clock didn't go off," "I didn't have time," "The customer made a mistake," "I can't get through to him on the phone," "The computer fouled up," "The economy is bad," and so forth. Never be caught speechless when it comes to making excuses for yourself.

2. NEVER STAND OUT FROM THE PACK   Losers know that it is important to be invisible. Vanilla is their favorite flavor. Never call attention to yourself. Look, act, and work the way you really are—mediocre.

3. KEEP YOUR EYE ON THE COMPETITION   Think and breathe the competition. Know all about them—their

weaknesses, their opportunities, their problems, and their needs. Never think about your customers.

4. AVOID TAKING RISKS AT ALL COST   Risk-taking is extremely dangerous. You may either fail or succeed. Either one will put you in great jeopardy. Risk-takers lead the pack by always wanting to test themselves. They're never satisfied with their performance—they want to do better. They welcome risks as opportunities. Such thinking makes you shudder.

5. NEVER LET YOURSELF BECOME ENTHUSIASTIC   If you do, you will want to do more, become more deeply involved in your work, and place your company, co-workers, and customers ahead of yourself.

6. ALWAYS PUT YOURSELF FIRST   Before you agree to anything, ask yourself this question: "What's in it for me?" If something requires extra time and effort, it could lead to more sales, increased productivity, and higher profits for your company. By putting yourself first, all these problems are avoided.

7. IF SOMETHING GOES WRONG, BLAME SOMEONE
This is very important. Taking responsibility causes difficulties, so make sure you always have someone in mind to blame when a problem arises. Taking responsibility only makes you more valuable. You may even come to be viewed as a leader.

8. SPEND A LOT OF TIME SECOND-GUESSING THE BOSS
This is your real job—a top priority. By never showing any initiative, you are guaranteed a permanent position—at the bottom of the ladder.

9. NEVER LEARN ANYTHING NEW   Knowledge is dangerous! It means you will become a problem-solver. If this hap-

pens, customers will view you as essential to their success and your company will give you regular promotions.

10. IF ALL ELSE FAILS, SAY, "I DON'T KNOW." The less you know, the better off you are. Whenever you're asked a question, just say, "I don't know." You will quickly become exactly what you are—useless.

Becoming a winner is easy. All you have to do is break these Ten Commandments.

———— ◇ ————

The Devil's Business Dictionary

(with Apologies to Ambrose Bierce)

If you're in business, you probably take pride in your no-nonsense, practical approach to almost everything. Your success comes from clear thinking, quick action, and shrewd dealings. You are where you are today because you have worked harder, taken more risks, and stayed with it when others faltered. All this sounds good to those of us who own or operate businesses. It's a well-deserved pat on the back that we give ourselves periodically.

Yet, it seems that those of us in business are also victims. We're suckers for our own baloney, seduced by our own nonsense words. In fact, our work-a-day vocabulary is filled with more junk than a dumpster the day after Christmas.

Here are some terms that should never be used again in business, especially in marketing literature or sales presentations. They all sound both profound and impressive, but they really mean nothing. If you see them in writing, cross them out.

If they are spoken in your presence, walk away. If you catch yourself using them, go sit in the corner and clear your mind.

Maybe we ought to be considering such words as integrity, responsibility, and quality. That, as we all know, is way, way downstream.

BOTTOM LINE   If you want a macho image in business, all you have to do is punctuate your speech—particularly to employees and business associates—with such phrases as "What's the impact on the bottom line?" or "All I'm interested in is the bottom line." This is the latest version of John Wayne out West. It sounds tough, tough, tough. And it doesn't mean a damn thing!

BURN-OUT   The close companion to this one is, of course, "stress." No wonder American business is taking such a beating in the world economy. We get our kicks out of pampering ourselves. Some firms even have "mental health" days for their employees. If anyone is suffering from mental fatigue it's the companies that provide for such B.S. We do a better and better job at making it clear that "hard work" is a dirty notion! We seem to be more interested in coddling ourselves than we are in determining our endurance, developing our ability to work under pressure, and to come out on top. If Thomas Edison had known about "burn-out," we'd still be sitting in the dark. Come to think of it, maybe we are.

CEO, CFO, COO, and CIO   Wow! Now, we're really in the big time. These initials work wonders. Just add them to the letterhead and business card and you're ten feet tall. Think of the power and prestige. You're not just the President, you're a step up and beyond—you're the CEO—whatever that means. But, watch out. There's something happening out there. Look out for the guy who is dissatisfied with just being the CEO. Before you know it, he's going for broke. He's about to become CEO, CFO,

COO, and CIO. The accumulation of titles is the game "kids" in business play to amuse themselves—and others.

COMFORT LEVEL   How soft can we get? Well, you can be sure we're working on it. This is just another of those goof-ball terms concocted by the "how-can-we-preserve-our-jobs" Human Resources people. All of a sudden, we're worried about whether or not Sally feels comfortable with her new responsibilities, when we ought to be asking ourselves a more appropriate question: "Can Sally really do the job?" "Don't move too fast," we're told. "We've got to be sure Sally feels comfortable with what's happening."

CUT A CHECK   This is by far the supreme insult. "Sure, Joe. I'll cut you a check." It sounds like the guy is going to chisel it out of granite. What kind of malarkey is this? The only people I've ever known to use "cut a check" are those who don't pay their bills. They can't bring themselves to say, "I'll have the check for you in the morning." Such directness drives them crazy. They fight it to the death before they pay. They'll do anything to avoid it—like saying, "I'll cut you a check." Or, more likely, they have no intention of paying you at all. As a result, they make it sound as if they are about to move all of Chase Manhattan into action—when, in fact, they aren't going to do a damned thing—including, pay you. Who says business isn't soft headed? Who says we're tough minded? Just listen to the way we talk and you'll get the message.

DOWNSIDE   This one really makes you sound "in charge." After you've listened to the presentation, the right thing to say goes something like this: "That sounds good, but what's the downside?" Now, you've got the poor so-and-so on the spot. You're ready to carve the turkey! You're going to shoot all those fresh, creative ideas full of holes the size of the Grand Canyon. That's why you get exactly what you deserve from the people around you—"Yes, sir," "No, sir," and "You're absolutely right, sir."

DOWNSTREAM   It's also time to be down on downstream. This is just another variation on hollow executive jargon. "Yes, that's a very good idea, but what are the implications downstream?" Didn't anyone ever let you know that this is a business and not a riverboat?

FULL-SERVICE   This is the most overused—and, therefore, meaningless, term in business. The people who add it to everything—letterhead, business cards, brochures, ads, and even invoices—seem to think they're saying something important. As a matter of fact, they aren't saying anything. Now, it is true that *full service* could have a distinct meaning—if there were *quarter-service, half-service,* and *three-quarters service* companies. If you can't express in some relevant way what you do, then it's time to turn the business over to someone who knows the score.

GET UP TO SPEED   This is a great one. It's ever so graphic, too. What does it mean? Easy. When someone says, "I'm getting up to speed on the project," there's a clear, distinct, and unavoidable message: "The project has been sitting on my desk for months. Now, I am being prodded, pushed, and prevailed upon, and it's about time to get it moving." It's baloney. It would be far more honest to say, "Frankly, I haven't looked at the damned thing yet. Give me a couple of days and I'll get caught up."

ENTREPRENEUR   Anyone doing anything is an entrepreneur today, including those who cannot pronounce the word. It has a touch of class, even though no one knows what it means. *Entrepreneur* is particularly popular among those who are super-cautious and monumentally unimaginative. It's also a form of flattery practiced by clever salespeople. "As an entrepreneur," they intone, "you know the value of... ." Don't be taken in by such silliness.

EXECUTIVE OFFICES   These are isolation suites created by top company officials so they can avoid anything that might disturb and interfere with their fantasies. These clever chambers are designed to insulate lofty figures from the marketplace, employees, customers,—and, particularly, complaints. Never go to work for any company that has the words "Executive Offices" on a door. The president will tell you his door is always open. Sounds great—until you have the unmitigated gaul to try to walk through it.

FAIR PRICE   The proposal concludes with—"We're giving it to you at a fair price." Fair to whom? Shouldn't the guy getting the proposal have a chance to evaluate if he thinks the price is fair? "Fair price" is nothing more than a monumental display of arrogance. And people who use it are generally unable to justify the price they're quoting. They simply think using the words solve all the problems. They don't. Worse yet, we use the term so often, we come to believe what we're saying.

HUMAN RESOURCES   Personnel Departments have always been a problem. Shoved off to the sidelines, these people "got no respect." And for good reason. To the guys at the top, they were a drag on the budget. In any smooth-running, successful organization, the personnel department was insignificant and unimportant—as it should be. Then, someone came up with the clever idea of changing the name to make the hoax more palatable. Now, on doors and business cards everywhere, the same useless folk in personnel are holding their heads high. Some have even had themselves elevated to "Vice President." Frankly, the term "Human Resources" connotes something impersonal, insensitive, aloof, and brutally calculating. That's progress?

233

LEVEL PLAYING FIELD   When it dawned on us that the Japanese were getting all the orders, business leaders rose out of their chairs in righteous indignation. No one dared to cry, "Foul." That would be *inappropriate* for those who proudly subscribe to the "It's a jungle out there" credo. Rather, they took what they thought was the high road of "fair play." What a picture! Deeply committed to rough-and-tumble competition, these captains of business began whining, "All we want is a level playing field." What do they really mean? We don't want anyone else to play in our sandbox.

MANAGEMENT COMMITTEE   This is one of the most appealing terms in business today. It sounds so contemporary—utilizing the human resources of the group to achieve more positive results. Actually, it's a technique created by management to avoid individual responsibility. If something goes wrong (and it always does), who can point a finger at a committee? Don't trust anyone who serves on a "Management Committee." Be very careful what you say in front of one of these people. And never, never put anything in writing. Remember, Management Committees have only one job—to point a finger at you.

OUTPLACEMENT   We not only have the word, but now we even have firms using it proudly in their corporate names. Who are we kidding? Certainly, not the victim of *outplacement*. We all know who these people are. They're fired. That's it. Fired. Say it 10 times and it's not so frightening. Of course we prefer something like outplacement. It's a euphemism. It makes the company feel better, less of the heavy. Actually *outplacement* may be rather accurate—we're placing them out on the street. It's time to be more honest with everybody—including ourselves.

POWER LUNCH   Watch out for anyone who thinks that where you eat is more important than what you eat. For them, being seen is the substance. These are people without taste and judgement. They follow trends faster than Superman can don his cape. They are T.S. Eliot's "hollow men"—their heads are filled with straw. They live by their wits and not their brains (they have too much of the former and not enough of the latter). Their biggest problem is finding a *power necktie* to wear to tomorrow's *power lunch*. Frankly, McDonald's is beginning to look pretty good.

REORGANIZATION   If you can't get up the nerve to *restructure,* (see next entry), there is a less painful alternative. *Reorganize.* This is simply a matter of moving the totally incompetent management team around on the organizational chart. This gives them each another year of gainful employment before someone screams "scam" and throws them out.

RESTRUCTURING   Here's a current *in* word. Everybody is doing it these days. It's the rage in the business world. "Hey, Tom. Have you heard? U.S. Doofrabitz is *restructuring.* We'd better get moving. The competition will get ahead of us." Just the sound of the word is impressive—*restructuring.* It seems to suggest something creative, innovative, and totally different is happening. It isn't, as we all know. All it means is that the company had better be cut down in size before it goes broke. It's time to stop *restructuring* and go to work.

SALES ENGINEER   This is nothing more than fantasy world language dreamed up by some dopey VP who thinks that both his sales force and his customers are stupid. For some unknown reason, this guy, who lacks self-confidence, has decided there's something undignified, unprofessional, and distressing with the term *salesman.* In the same way, he thinks the term *engineer* will leave the prospect in utter awe. What moves the would-be customer is competence and knowledge—and you can't put that on a business card.

STATE OF THE ART   When was the last time you tried to make a copy on a state-of-the-art copier or get hold of the engineering department on a state-of-the-art telephone? Neither is possible. Both are filled with features nobody wants, needs, or is capable of using. State-of-the-art is an illusion foisted on us by irresponsible marketing departments and subscribed to by salespeople who have been on the job just long enough to read the latest marketing brochure.

SYSTEM   If anything is going to sell today, it had better be a *system*. The state-of-the-art copier is now a state-of-the-art *copying system*. Are the copies any better? Of course not. But the annual service contract is five times more than last year's model. Just add the word *system* to whatever you're doing, selling, or manufacturing and you'll have a license to hike the price.

TELEMARKETING   This is one word that epitomizes what's wrong with business today. No one can simply call a customer or talk to a prospect on the phone. Everything must be *telemarketing*. What it implies is the specific effort to abuse, dehumanize, and overwhelm the person who has the ill fortune of being on the other end of the line. The *script* is everything. Just get the right response. Nothing else matters—including truth or the needs of the customer. The most efficient *telemarketing* is calculated to avoid building a relationship and is most successful when it maximizes manipulation. It's time to rethink how we approach both customers and prospects. Perhaps their negative responses are the direct result of being bombarded by *"telemarketing"* pros who are anything but professional.

WINDOW OF OPPORTUNITY   Here's a real winner. It's used so often today, you come to the conclusion that there's something magic about the phrase. But what in the world is a *window of opportunity*? Is it a hole in the ozone layer? Is it something that lets in light? Or, perhaps, you jump through it from the 20th floor? Actually, *window of opportunity* is the "sure thing." If we miss it now, it will never happen again. It's all emotion. It's exciting. It's a way to make the blood race through our veins. But, before you get too excited, just remember that old Peoria proverb—"People who jump through windows of opportunity never land on their feet."

Index